Growing to Maturity
A Messianic Jewish Guide
Third Edition

Daniel C. Juster

Union of Messianic Jewish Congregations
Denver • Colorado

The Union of Messianic Jewish Congregations Press
Denver, Colorado
© 1982, © 1985, © 1987 by Daniel C. Juster
Third Edition published in 1987
Printed in the United States of America

95   94   93   92   6   5   4   3
Library of Congress Catalog Card Number
85-050301

ISBN 0-9614555-0-0

Union of Messianic Jewish Congregations
8556 East Warren Avenue
Denver, Colorado 80231-3337
(303) 337-4324
(303) 337-6254

Published at the direction and under the supervision of the
Union of Messianic Jewish Congregations.

Cover Illustration: High Holy Days

Set in 10 point Camelot with 2 points of lead at the REF
Typesetting & Publishing Center, Manassas, Virginia 22110.

All Scripture quotations are from the *New International
Version* of the Bible.

DEDICATION

Since this is a book on discipleship the author wished to acknowledge those who have had the greatest mark upon his discipling.

Foremost is the late Chaplin Evan D. Welsh of Wheaton College, my spiritual father; Dr. David L. Wolfe of Gorden College; Dr. Stuart C. Hackett of Trinity Evangelical Divinity School and Dr. Kenneth S. Kantzer of Trinity as well. They were my mentors in integrating faith and learning.

TABLE OF CONTENTS

GROWING TO MATURITY GUIDE

FOR DISCIPLERS USING THIS BOOK

Discipling is one of the most important functions of a congregation. Yeshua said, "Go and make disciples." A disciple is someone who has learned to be like the Master in essential spiritual and moral qualities. It is someone who lives according to the lifestyle exemplified and taught by Yeshua and His disciples. Discipling is therefore not merely imparting intellectual knowledge, but helping a person live rightly.

The discipler is one who gives his life in care for the disciple. This involves several important things:

1. Meeting regularly for Bible study.
2. Keeping regular contact to show care and personal interest.
3. Praying with and for the disciple, that he may come to maturity of faith.
4. Exhorting and lovingly correcting the disciple.
5. Spending time with the disciple in your home so he may observe the lifestyle of believers.
6. Seeing that the disciple gets to know personally a variety of mature believers in the congregation; establishing him in fellowship and regular participation in the congregation.

The disciple is your special responsibility; your goal is that he becomes a committed part of the congregation and receives direct leadership from the elders; and even then you should maintain a special relationship with the disciple. As the disciple grows in the Lord you should help him to:

1. Be *consistent in having a regular quiet time* and developing a real love relationship with the Lord.
2. *Grow out of problems* through biblical solutions.
3. *Discover his primary gift motivation* and secondary gifts. This leads to helping him find his area(s) of service in the body according to a prayerful response to God's Spirit.
4. Adopt a life style of obedience to God.

A big problem for many people in their service to the Lord is *time management.* They simply do not organize their priorities according to the values of God's kingdom. Instead of praying about how to spend time, most people are creatures of impulsive responses and end up producing little of value for the Lord. This is a central area in which the discipler can help and care for the disciple. The discipline of quiet time is a first key in this regard.

USING THE DISCIPLESHIP SERIES

The discipler should meet with his disciple weekly or even more often until the discipleship course is complete. Meeting at the same time every week is a big help in developing consistency and discipline.

The discipleship course is divided into eight chapters with three sections in each. At times these sections are divided into subsections. Italicized material denotes things which the disciple should particularly remember. After each of the 24 sections you will find study questions and verses for memorization. This is to help both you and the disciple. It helps provide an outline for the weekly discussion. The study questions can also be discussed and a test of the memorized verses given.

A typical session might include:

1. Finding out how the disciple is doing.
   Has he established a daily quiet time?

This is important. Also discuss any concerns the disciple might have.
2. Praying together before the lesson.
3. Going over the material for the week by:
   a. Reviewing the main points in the booklets.
   b. Discussing study questions.
4. Testing memorization of verses.
5. Having a period of prayer together. Teaching by example that the disciple should learn to really seek God in prayer.

For the disciple reinforcement in learning is provided by:
1. Reading the sections.
2. Answering the study questions.
3. Memorizing verses connected to the section.
4. Discussing with the discipler:
   a. The material in general,
   b. Any questions,
   c. Any further explanations,
   d. The study questions and memorization verses.

For the discipler, the outline and main points provide an order of presentation while also seeing to it the disciple has accomplished the goals within the book (e.g., confession, forgiveness, quiet time, body life, etc.). Step by step the disciple will be adding to his life the basic building blocks of a fully biblical lifestyle.

If the disciple has answered the questions, seems to understand the basics, and is in accord with the basic flow of a biblical lifestyle, he is ready to be formally received by the congregation if this is the routine of the community. If not, he can be seen as ready to take his full place as a committed member. *Memorizing the verses is a real key.* The disciple should be encouraged to make memory cards. This is a lifetime task. The discipleship course is only a beginning of the discipline of Scripture memorization.

The key to true discipleship always comes down to love—love expressed in caring for, praying for, praying with, and spending time with the disciple. May God give you lasting fruit in discipling.

MESSIANIC JEWISH DISCIPLESHIP

Daniel Juster

INTRODUCTION: THE NATURE OF DISCIPLESHIP

Yeshua said, "Go and make disciples." A disciple is someone who is like the Master Himself. Yeshua's command is the first reason for discipleship. Our concern is that Jewish followers of the Messiah be *under His Lordship*, be *grounded in the Word*, and *know the truth* and *live by the truth* as it is revealed in Scripture.

Discipleship is a lifestyle of "walking in His steps." It is a life of godly service, prayer, and fellowship in the household of faith. Therefore, this series of lessons is only a first step in discipleship. Let us press on in knowing the Lord and living in the constant presence of the Spirit.

Yeshua said, "Why do you call me Lord, and not do what I say?" (Luke 6:46). In Matthew 7, He makes it clear that accepting His salvation means yielding our lives without reservation. We may not know the total will of the Lord, but "Not everyone who says 'Lord, Lord,' shall enter into the kingdom of heaven, but he that does the will of my Father." Salvation is by God's grace; a person who truly accepts God's grace is willing and able to do God's will.

This discipleship series presents these first steps of understanding and spiritual practice tailored to the Jewish believer. It hopefully will be an aid in living according to Yeshua's will as a disciple, one who has learned the example of his teacher.

THE METHOD OF THIS BOOK

The discipleship book you are using in this course is structured according to recent advances in individualized educational instruction. Discipleship is serious business and this material is geared for serious study and reflection.

Each chapter is divided into short sections followed by study questions. These questions are to be answered in the book. Memory verses are assigned after the study questions. These should be written on index cards and memorized. They are key aids to building faith and maturity. After answering the sectional study questions, you should check your answers by the italicized portions of the text.

Following Yeshua is a new world; there is a new language to be learned and new ways of thinking. Learning is crucial to real discipleship.

ACKNOWLEDGMENTS

Special thanks to Johanna Chernoff who supplied helpful material on holiness, praise, and community life. We also acknowledge many other discipleship materials (e.g., Navigators, Derek Prince's *Foundations*). Certainly this course builds from them, although we no longer can recall the exact origin of all the ideas.

We assume all who enter this course have been through the booklet *L'Hayim* (to life) and had it clearly explained. This needs to be understood before moving on to this course.

THE PLAN OF SALVATION

1. THE PLAN OF SALVATION
GENERAL OVERVIEW OF OUR COURSE OF STUDY

The goal of this section is to give a basic understanding of God's plan of salvation for the individual and for humanity. First of all, you will learn the definitions of basic biblical terms, and secondly, you will memorize a basic set of Scripture passages to enable you to be grounded in these truths.

SECTION A—CREATION TO ABRAHAM

The Scriptures tell us, "In the beginning God created the heavens and the earth" (Genesis 1:1). The biblical description of God is a description of an infinite being of unlimited intelligence and moral perfection. Only Scripture gives the revelation of a personal, infinite God. To say *God is personal* means He has real attributes of self-consciousness, intelligence, will, and the ability to act, love, judge, and relate to other people in special ways.

Let's look at some Scripture passages which reveal what God is like:

> "And He passed in front of Moses, proclaiming, 'The Lord, the Lord, the compassionate and gracious God, slow to anger, abounding in love and faithfulness, maintaining love to thousands, and forgiving wickedness, rebellion and sin. Yet He does not leave the guilty unpunished; He punishes the children and their children for the sin of the fathers to the third and fourth generation.' " (Exodus 34:6,7)

Leviticus 19:2 says, "Speak to the entire assembly of Israel and say to them: 'Be holy because I, the Lord your God, am holy' ".

The first passage is known in traditional Judaism as the 13 attributes of God. In it we see that although God is full of love and mercy, He must punish sin, for He is just. The sin of one generation has clear effects on the next, as is all too clear today.

God is *holy*. That is, He is *totally separated from evil, uncleanliness,* and *immoral ways.* He is full of love and compassion.

Leviticus 19:1 brings up the human dilemma and need for salvation. The Bible teaches God is perfect and requires perfect righteousness in those with whom He fellowships. Yet every human being finds his life is full of sin. *To sin* (Chat' in Hebrew) *means* to *miss the mark,* the mark of God's perfect standard. There is the awful sense of distance from God; separation from our creator. How did we get in this state and how do we get out of it?

In Genesis two, we see God created man *in His own image.* To be created in God's *image* means to be a *reflection of God in function and attributes.* Man was created to function, as God, as a ruler over this earth (Gen.1:26,27). To perform this function, he was given dominion. He was also given attributes like God; abilities such as love, intelligence, freedom, and intuition. God created man for loving fellowship with Himself.

If man was to be a morally significant companion for God, he had to have a real choice. He was placed in a garden of abundance and told to enjoy the fruit of the garden with one exception. The exception was that he was not to eat of the tree of the knowledge of good and evil which would give him the experiential knowledge of evil.

But under the influence of the devil, first the woman, and then the man did eat. They were tempted by vanity and pride. They wanted to become like God. They asserted their independence from God with disastrous results. God had warned Adam and Eve that eating from this tree, an act of rebellion, would bring both spiritual and physical death. This was indeed the consequence, because after disobeying God, the human parents of our race knew lust, greed, anger, and other manifestations of selfishness. *Selfishness* is when self and its desires are enthroned as lord of our lives instead of God.

The human race is of one fabric; the life of the children is tied to the life of the parents. A nature bent toward sin and selfishness was thus passed on to all of us. In Genesis four, Cain killed his brother Abel. By Genesis six the whole human race was so given over to evil that it was almost completely destroyed by a flood. The Bible is realistic about the central human disease, sin. It recognizes the root of the problem as self-centeredness and rebellion against God. But God allowed the human race to continue. Why? Was it possible that man could be *redeemed, purchased back* from his state of spiritual death (separation from God) and eventual physical death? Wonderfully, the answer is yes.

God's plan of salvation centered first on a chosen nation. This plan began with Abraham. Abraham submitted himself to serve the living God; he obeyed God's call and moved to a new land to begin a new nation. God called Abraham His friend (Isaiah 41:8). He gave him great promises. He told him:

1. He would make of him a mighty *nation* (Genesis 12:2,3),
2. He would make his *seed* a source of blessing to all nations,
3. He would give Abraham's descendants (through Jacob) the *land* of Israel, and
4. He would *bless* those who bless Israel, and curse those who curse Israel.

God supernaturally produced a child named Isaac through Abraham and Sarah in that they were well beyond childbearing age. Later Abraham's descendants were rescued from Egypt and brought into the promised land. God decided to win the human race back to Himself through a nation. This nation was to be submitted to God's will, an example of righteousness, a witness to God's ways. Israel was to be an instrument of God's justice and the image of a redeemed community. They would call the other nations back to God.

Some questions may arise at this point. Was Abraham sinless? Wasn't he a part of fallen humanity? Why could he be accepted into fellowship with God? How could his descendants and eventually other members of the human race be accepted by God? The complete answer to these questions is not given until the New Covenant Scriptures (New Testament). But a partial answer is given.

First we see that "Abraham believed the Lord, and He reckoned (credited) it to him as righteousness" (Genesis 15:6). Somehow faith, believing trust in God, is capable of making us acceptable to God. Abraham was not perfect, he still fell from God's high standard. At one point out of fear he asked Sarah to pretend that she was not his wife (Genesis 12:10ff). He also sought to produce a child by his own efforts, through Sarah's handmaid Hagar, to assure himself of descendants. Yet his basic faith in God remained and produced great responses of obedience as well (Romans 4).

The greatest test of Abraham's faith was when God called him to sacrifice his only son, Isaac (Genesis 22). Just before he raised the knife to slay Isaac, God stopped him. To have gone through with God's instructions to this extent was as good as carrying them out completely. Truly he gave all to God. But why did God command Abraham to slay his only son of miraculous birth? Why did he seek an image of sacrifice in the son in whom was the promise of blessing? Jewish tradition, in Talmud and the Siddur (Prayer book), gives added meaning to the sacrifice of Isaac. Since we are in Isaac, tied to him as descendants, the prayer is offered that God might remember this sacrifice and forgive our sins. Somehow our forgiveness is tied to sacrifice, someone paying a great penalty for us and having merit which counts as our own.

Faith and sacrifice are part of God's means of restoring us to Himself. How this works is part of the next section.

STUDY QUESTIONS

1. Define what it means to say *God is personal* or a person.

   _____

2. Define the meaning of *holy.* _____

   _____

3. What does it mean to be created in *God's image?* _____

   _____

4. Define selfishness biblically. _____

   _____

5. "To purchase back" is Scriptually called: _____

   _____

6. What were four of God's promises to Abraham?

   a. _____

   b. _____

   c. _____

   d. _____

7. What are two key elements for restoration to fellowship with God according to the accounts of Abraham's life?

   a. _____ b. _____

VERSES FOR MEMORIZATION

Learn both the verse and the reference. (Repeat the reference before and after quoting the verse, e.g., John 1:12 the text . . . John 1:12)

Genesis 15:6   Exodus 34:6,7

SECTION B—ISRAEL
LAW, PRIESTHOOD, AND SACRIFICE

The descendants of Abraham through Jacob were called Israelites due to Jacob's name change. *Israel* is one who prevails with God, TO STRIVE WITH GOD as a prince. At the time of God's visitation through Moses, Israel was in a sorry state. She had sunk into the meanest bondage under cruel Egyptian overseers. But God brought Israel out of Egypt with a "mighty hand and outstretched arm." God rescued a nation of slaves to indicate His love for all who are poor and dispossessed, whose situation is hopeless.

In the plagues He cast upon Egypt, God defeated not only the will of the nation, but their trust in their own gods and religious figures who were supposed to protect them. If Egypt were the most powerful nation of its day, the defeat of the nation by a multitude of unarmed slaves certainly proved the supremacy of the God of these slaves. Almost every plague was a defeat of a particular Egyptian god. The defeat of the highest god, the sun god, was shown in the plague of darkness and in the death of Pharoah's firstborn son who was thought to be a direct descendant of the sun god. God demonstrated His universal Lordship over all nations in His defeat of Egypt.

Many are familiar with the story of Passover itself (Exodus 12). On that evening the angel of death passed over the houses of Israel, but in the Egyptians' homes He killed all the firstborn sons. The angel of death passed over all the homes which displayed the blood of a lamb on the doorposts and lintel. Once again sacrifice, a blood offering, is shown as necessary in averting judgment.

Israel's deliverance from Egypt and possession of the land of Canaan is the foundational image of all salvation. First of all, it should be noted that Israel was absolutely helpless in saving herself. There was nothing she could do to defeat the armies of Pharoah or get to the other side of the sea when she was totally hemmed in. Her defeat of the Canaanites and entrance into the promised land was by God's mighty power. Israel did not triumph because of her ability with the sword, although God allowed her to use the sword. She triumphed by faith! Similar principles are evident in Israel's conquering Jericho. She walked around the walls of Jericho and the walls came tumbling down. Note these elements in Israel's salvation:

1. She could not save herself; no work of her own was adequate. Her salvation was an act of God.
2. She was only able to receive her deliverance when she acted by faith. In faith and obedience she marched through the sea (Exodus 14). Later in faith and obedience Israel surrounded Jericho. She shouted and the power of God destroyed the walls of the city.
3. The blood sacrifice averted the judgment of God. Only after the angel of death passed over the blood-stained homes of Israel could she respond in faith to God's demonstration of power and march out of Egypt.

It's the same with us. We cannot save ourselves. We can only respond in faith to God's act of salvation; we require a blood sacrifice to free us from judgment. The Exodus gives us an image of salvation and foreshadows the salvation which all human beings can find in Yeshua. Salvation is deliverance from the bondage of slavery to sin and entrance into the promised land of eternal life with God.

Before Israel entered into the promised land she was given the Mosaic constitution to govern her life as a nation. This constitutional material makes up a good portion of the Torah, the five books of Scripture written by the hand of Moses. Central in the Torah is material which reflects God's universal moral standards, such as the Ten Commandments (Exodus 20) and the Shema (Deuteronomy 6:4ff). The Shema (from the Hebrew word to hear or heed) says:

"Hear, O Israel: The Lord our God, the Lord is one.
Thou shalt love the Lord your God with all your heart
and with all your soul and with all your strength."

Yeshua said this is the greatest commandment. The second greatest, He taught, is like unto it, namely Leviticus 19:34 which commands us to love our neighbor as ourselves (see Mark 12:29-32).

(The student should take a moment here to read the Ten Commandments in Exodus 20.)

These commandments do not exhaust the universal moral and social standards of God reflected in the Torah. These standards call for business honesty, justice in the courts, and concern for the fatherless, the widowed, the alien and the poor.

The Torah also contains laws which enabled Israel to adjust to life 3400 years ago with accommodations to their limited abilities and the limitations of the age. There is also revelation of a Temple-sacrificial system under the oversight of an inherited priesthood. Also included were days of memory to root the nation in what God had done for them; rescuing, establishing, and providing for them.

For now, we want to zero in on the moral law reflected in the Torah. No one can honestly say he or she has perfectly fulfilled the standards of the Torah. When we read the Ten Commandments reflectively, we know even if we have not externally cursed, committed adultery, or stolen, we have had the seeds of these things in our hearts. Torah says, "Do not hate your brother *in your heart*" (Leviticus 19:17).

Yeshua taught that "to hate" is "to murder in the heart." So it is with lustful desires. Or can anyone say they have perfectly honored their parents? Who among us is free from coveting, which is a greedy desire for possessions, or for the blessings given to someone else? Certainly when we hear the command to love God with all our heart, soul, strength, and might, and our neighbors as ourselves, we are undone! Before God's holy and perfect law, we stand condemned.

The Scripture pronounces a curse on *all* who do not live according to all the words of Torah (Deuteronomy 28:15-68). Through the Torah we become aware of our utter distance from God's holy perfection. Scripture makes it absolutely clear that no amount of our own good deeds can redeem us from (buy us out of) this situation. We read in Isaiah 64:6,

> "All of us have become like one who is unclean, and all our righteous acts (good deeds) are like filthy rags . . . ."

We also read in Psalm 143:2,

> "Do not bring your servant into judgment, for no one living is righteous before you."

Scripture teaches that joy and fulfillment in life are only possible through fellowship with God. "You will fill me with joy in Your presence, with eternal pleasures at Your right hand." (Psalm 16:11). We need to know God. On the other hand we read, "But your iniquities have separated you from your God; your sins have hidden His face from you."(Isaiah 59:2).

This is why every holy man falls on his face in the presence of God's holiness. Isaiah pleaded for God to depart from him for he said he was a man of unclean lips. Isaiah fell on the ground and cried "Woe to me." (Isaiah 6:5).

We get no adequate concept of our desperate need until we recognize our utter distance from acceptability before God. I used to think of my good deeds as outweighing my bad deeds. If the scale tipped in my favor, I would be acceptable to God. This is a wrong concept, although one commonly held by many who call themselves Christians and Jews.

THE WRONG CONCEPT OF ACCEPTANCE BEFORE GOD

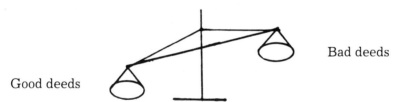

Bad deeds

Good deeds

The good deeds outweigh the bad.
Therefore righteous before God.

THE TRUE TEST IS THE SUM IN PERFECTION

OF OUR LIFE COMPARED TO GOD'S STANDARD

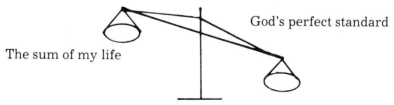

God's perfect standard

The sum of my life

The scale is always balanced against me.
I am condemned.

We tend to compare ourselves to other people and say. "I'm not so bad, I'm okay." But this is false reason for comfort. Let's say two people compete in jumping for distance. One is an average person; he jumps six feet. The other is an Olympian and jumps 23 feet. The Olympian could feel good about his 23-foot jump. However, it would do him no good if he was trapped by a forest fire and had to jump a 1000-foot canyon to escape. The six-foot jumper and the 23-foot jumper would both be condemned to die in the flames. This is our spiritual state before the holy perfection of God. There has to be another way of acceptance before God. Once again the concepts of God's act of saving, faith, and sacrifice, come to the foreground. The ancient Israelite was given a means to cover his sin before God in the old temple sacrifice.

We read these remarkable words in Leviticus 17:11:

> "For the life of a creature is in the blood, and I have given it to you to make atonement for yourselves on the altar; *it is the blood* that makes atonement for one's life."

When the ancient Israelite transgressed God's law, he brought a sacrifice, an unblemished animal, to the priest. He laid his hand upon the animal's head and confessed his sin. This was an act of owning up, of admitting he deserved the penalty the animal was about to receive. His sin was symbolically *transferred to the animal* which was *slain in his place*. The Israelite priest then swallowed the part of the sacrifice not consumed by fire, dissolving the existence of sin and guilt in his own body (see Leviticus 1-7).

The animal represented the Israelite symbolically. In the guilt offering, guilt was dissolved. The burnt offering, completely burned unto God, symbolized the full rededication of the offerer to God; he would now live totally unto God. The blood of the sacrifice covered his sin and provided atonement (covering for sin).

We see this blood sacrifice for the families of Israel in Passover and for the individual in Leviticus chapters one through seven.

We see that the high priest represented all the people and killed the lamb of sacrifice for them on Yom Kippur. Only the high priest was privileged to enter the Holy of Holies where the very presence of God was found in ancient Israel. In this inner room of the temple, the priest provided the blood of atonement for the whole nation.

The temple sacrifice pointed to the need for a mediator between God and man. The priest in his holy robes and beautiful jewelry represented the majestic holy God before the people. However, when he stood before God, he was the representative of the people, making sacrifice for them and swallowing their sin as he ate the sacrifice. This was true of the high priest and of the others who officiated.

The sacrifices represented four central elements: 1) *the holiness of God in His hatred of sin*; 2) *the destructiveness of sin pictured in the animal's death*; 3) *the need for owning up to sin and a substitute sacrifice*; and 4) *the mercy of God* who pardons sinners. The whole of Ancient Israel's religion is *filled with the concept of the need for a mediator and a sacrifice.*

The ancient Israelite was restored to God by *faith in God's provision of a sacrificial lamb whose blood atoned for his sins.* God provided the way of escape by His mercy and grace (Hebrew-Hesed) and we respond in faith. Once again we see the *three elements of salvation: God's act to save us in our helplessness, faith in God and His provision, and the blood of a sacrifice.*

However, does the blood of bulls and goats really remove sin (Hebrews 10:11)? Or was the ancient Israelite participating in heavenly realities of the future without full understanding? Was the sacrificial system only a symbol and a way of participating in the true means of salvation?

The book of Hebrews answers these questions. Today there is no temple sacrifice system, but we still have the means of blood atonement through our great high priest, the Messiah Yeshua. Without Him, we do not have or know of the means of our acceptance with God. An understanding of His role answers the question of how a holy God can accept us, imperfect sinful creatures that we are, and make us new creatures in the Messiah (II Corinthians 5:17).

STUDY QUESTIONS

1. Define the meaning of the name Israel.
   _____

2. What are three central elements reflected in Israel's salvation from Egypt which show God's way of restoring fellowship with human beings?

   a. _____

   b. _____

   c. _____

3. The Torah is _____
4. The Central two commandments of Israel's faith as taught by Yeshua are:

   a. _____

   b. _____
5. According to Isaiah 64:5 and Psalm 143:2, describe man's problem in relation to his acceptance by God and good deeds.

   _____

   _____

6. What are four central elements reflected in the temple sacrifice?

   a. _____

   b. _____

   c. _____

   d. _____

VERSES FOR MEMORIZATION
1. Deuteronomy 6:4,5   2. Isaiah 64:5   3. Psalm 16:11

SECTION C
GOD'S PROVISION THROUGH THE MESSIAH

The Scriptures make it clear God's ultimate provision for reconciling human beings to Himself is through Israel's King and representative, the Messiah. *The words of the prophets give us an understanding of the Messiah's work for Israel and all mankind. The prophets also give us the characteristics by which we can recognize who the Messiah is.* As we trace the Messianic hope in the Tenach (Old Testament Scriptures), the student will perceive glorious truths. It is through the Messiah that Israel fulfills her role.

In Genesis 3:15 we read the seed of the woman will be wounded in the heel by the serpent, the personification of evil we know as the devil. However, He shall bruise the head of the devil. He shall inflict the mortal wound. It is interesting that the Messiah is said to be only the seed "of a woman" not "of a man" (Galatians 4:4).

In Genesis 22, we read about Isaac, the only son of God's promise, and see that he is nearly offered as a sacrifice.

We also read that the Messianic king will be born in Bethlehem (Micah 5:2), of a virgin (Isaiah 7:14), and will have a supernatural divine nature. Isaiah 9:6,7 says of the Messianic king:

> "For to us a child is born, to us a son is given, and the government will be on His shoulder. And He will be called Wonderful Counselor, Mighty God, Everlasting Father, Prince of Peace. Of the increase of His government and peace there will be no end."

However, the prophets make it clear His first and primary task will be to lay down His life as a sacrifice for sin (Psalm 22, Isaiah 53).

Our people expected the Messiah, son of David, to rule and bring God's kingdom of peace. He will yet do this. However, Scripture also shows He must give up his life before He reigns. The New Covenant Scriptures make it clear there will be a time lapse between His fulfillment of the Scriptures pointing to His suffering and death, and His fulfillment of the Scriptures predicting His reign of peace over all the earth.

The most wonderful description of the Messiah's work of sacrifice is found in Isaiah 53.

(The student should now carefully read this passage: Isaiah 52:13-53:12.)

"See, my servant will act wisely, He will be raised and lifted up and highly exalted. Just as there were many who were appalled at Him—His appearance was so disfigured beyond that of any man and His form marred beyond human likeness—So will He sprinkle many nations, and kings will shut their mouths because of Him. For what they were not told, they will see, and what they have not heard, they will understand. Who has believed our message and to whom has the arm of the Lord been revealed? He grew up before Him like a tender shoot, and like a root out of dry ground. He had no beauty or majesty to attract us to Him, nothing in His appearance that we should desire Him. He was despised and rejected by men, a man of sorrows, and familiar with suffering. Like one from whom men hide their faces He was despised, and we esteemed Him not. Surely He took up our infirmities and carried our sorrows, yet we considered Him stricken by God, smitten by Him, and afflicted. But He was pierced for our transgressions, He was crushed for our iniquities; the punishment that brought us peace was upon Him, and by His wounds we are healed. We all, like sheep, have gone astray, each of us has turned to his own way; and the Lord has laid on Him the iniquity of us all. He was oppressed and afflicted, yet He did not open His mouth; He was led like a lamb to the slaughter, and as a sheep before her shearers is silent, so He did not open His mouth. By oppression and judgment, He was taken away. And who can speak of His descendants? For He was cut off from the land of the living; for the transgression of my people He was stricken. He was assigned a grave with the wicked, and with the rich in His death, though He had done no violence, nor was any deceit in His mouth. Yet it was the Lord's will to crush him and cause him to suffer, and though the Lord makes His life a guilt offering, He will see His offspring and prolong His days, and the will of the Lord will prosper in His hand. After the suffering of His soul, He will see the light of life and be satisfied; by His knowledge my righteous servant will justify many, and He will bear their iniquities. Therefore I will give Him a portion among the great, and He will divide the spoils with the strong, because He poured out His life unto death, and was numbered with the transgressors. For He bore the sin of many, and made intercession for the transgressors.

In this passage we read that the report of the arm of the Lord's work will not be believed by the nation of Israel. He will be despised and rejected by men and not esteemed by Israel, who would consider Him smitten of God and afflicted (vv 53:3,4). However, He bore our sorrows, was crushed for our iniquities, and healed us by His wounds. Isaiah says:

"We all, like sheep, have gone astray, each of us has turned to his own way; and the Lord has laid on Him the iniquity of us all."

He was taken as a sheep to the slaughter and was silent before his oppressors. We read His death is with the wicked, yet He is with a rich man in his death (v. 53:9). In the New Testament we read Yeshua died between two thieves and then was removed from the cross by the rich man, Joseph of Aramathea (Matthew 27:38,57-60).

And yet, although He was an offering for sin and died as a sacrifice (v. 53:10), in the same verse we read He is alive, seeing His spiritual offspring and prolonging His days. This is a reference to His resurrection from the dead.

The conclusion in verse 11 is wonderful:

"By His knowledge my righteous servant will justify (cause to be accepted as righteous) many, and He will bear their iniquities."

Psalm 22 describes the Messiah's death by crucifixion. He is pierced in His hands and feet (v. 16).

In the pages of the New Testament we find four portraits of Yeshua (Jesus) the Messiah (Matthew, Mark, Luke, and John). These excellent first century accounts by His followers describe His fulfillment of the Old Testament Scriptures. The descriptions of His life, death and resurrection make it clear that He indeed is the promised Messiah.

At this point it is our task to answer a major question. How is it Yeshua's life, death, and resurrection, is the means of making us right with God? To understand this it is necessary to explain the concepts of *representation, fulfillment, salvation, the new covenant*, and *the body of believers as God's new community*. Of course later lessons more fully cover these explanations, but they are mentioned now with an eye to understanding God's plan of salvation. Let's turn our attention to the glorious teaching of the New Testament.

Scripture teaches the human race is a family, a wholistic reality which is more than the sum of its parts. Although each of us has an individual dimension of consciousness, responsibility, and worth, we are at the same time part of one another, making up the single fabric of the human race. We are part of a fallen human race. We are part of Adam. His fallen nature is also ours. We read "in Adam all died" (Romans 5:12,17,18). Although our foolish individualism would deny it, Scripture is clear; we are all of one fabric. Truly no man is an island.

Therefore the entire human race stands condemned in Adam. Furthermore, Adam is the *representative head* of the human race. He represented us in his sin. Of course every human being since Adam has individually confirmed his identity in Adam by disobeying God's will and breaking His law.

In contrast to this, we read about Yeshua:

"For God so loved the world that He gave His one and only Son, that whoever believes in Him shall not perish but have eternal life. For God did not send His Son into the world to condemn the world, but to save the world through Him." (John 3:16,17)

How is the world saved through Yeshua? It is saved because Yeshua was born as a man, yet He was totally perfect. He is sinless. Not only is He a child of man through Miriam (Mary), but He is the special Son of God—a special product of God's Spirit who came upon His earthly mother to enable the supernatural formation of a child in her womb. Yeshua was thus a child of man, but had no human father. He is a special Son of God. Thus He was able to be the true mediator between God and man (I Timothy 2:5). As a perfect man, He is destined to become the new representative head of our race. We would be tied to him. He is the mediator, the priesthood pointed to in the law.

Yeshua lived a perfect life of love according to the spirit of God's law. He taught the full meaning of the law by bringing out its true intent and clarifying the very height of God's will and standard of perfection (Matthew 5-7). Since He brought the very presence of God and His kingdom, the forces of evil receded before Him. He healed the deaf, blind, and leprous; He even raised the dead (John 11).

But it was the "will of the Lord to bruise Him." Evil rejected the shining love He demonstrated, and He laid down His life with forgiveness on His lips for those who abused Him. This is how He showed the true nature of God's love. He was delivered up by the rulers of ancient Israel to Pilate, the Roman governor. He was crucified on a cruel Roman instrument of death, a cross. And yet He said, "Father, forgive them, for they do not know what they are doing." (Luke 23:24).

But it was not possible for death to hold Him. On the third day, He rose from the dead (Matthew 28, Mark 16, Luke 24, John 20).

Yeshua died as a sacrifice for our sins. He rose again that we might have a sure hope. As Israel's king and representative and as the representative of the whole human race, He performed for us what we could not do for ourselves. He lived a perfect life according to the Law of God, He died for our sins in a representative connection with our race, and He rose from the dead.

When we receive Yeshua *by faith*, we are transferred from Adam's representation to His. We become spiritually connected

to Him and are in Him. Here again are the three elements of
salvation seen before:

1. *We cannot save ourselves. God must provide* the means
   of our salvation.
2. *Yeshua is God's provision* for our deliverance, deliverance from sin and separation from God. He is the sacrifice of God.
3. *We, by faith in God's provision*, receive deliverance or
   are saved. We come into a new relationship with God.
   We are accounted righteous.

When we receive Yeshua by faith, we are said to be, "In
Him." This act of believing or placing our trust in Him is spiritual rebirth or being born again. Yeshua said, "I tell you the
truth, unless a man is born again, he cannot see the kingdom of
God." (John 3:3).

Ezekiel 36 predicted this new birth as part of God's New
Covenant. The new birth is described in these terms (36:25-27):
God revives our inner spirit or gives us a new spirit, puts His
Holy Spirit in us, and moves us to obey His will or law. Jere-
miah 31:31ff describes this as God writing His law on our hearts
in the New Covenant.

An animal can only die in our place as a symbol. Yeshua
could really die for us because He was part of us. When we
receive Him, we are judged by God in Him. God does not do
away with His holy standard which would deny His own holy
nature. Rather, He makes a provision for us to be accounted
righteous according to His law in Yeshua. When we are "in
Him," we are considered:

1. Perfect according to the law in Him;
2. To have died for (and to) our sins in Him;
3. To have risen to new spiritual life in Him.

Furthermore, because Yeshua's life is now in us by the
Holy Spirit, we have the power to become progressively more
like the Messiah in love and goodness. This is the meaning of
salvation by grace. *Salvation by grace through faith* is the

means by which God freely provides a way for us to be accounted as righteous according to His law. This means of grace is the death and resurrection of Yeshua. It is received by faith.

> "For it is by grace you have been saved, through faith-and this is not from yourselves, it is the gift of God-not by works, so that no one can boast. For we are God's workmanship, created in Messiah Yeshua to do good works. . . ." (Ephesians 2:8-10)

How do we receive Yeshua by faith? The best way is to express inner conviction by verbally turning your life over to God and telling Him you receive Yeshua and His salvation. Romans 10:9,10 says,

> "That if you confess with your mouth, 'Yeshua is Lord,' and believe in your heart that God raised Him from the dead, you will be saved. . . and it is with your mouth that you confess and are saved."

Confessing with your mouth makes this salvation real.

Salvation is deliverance *from separation from God unto life and fellowship with God.* It includes these wonderful blessings:

1. Answered prayer—God hears us and we hear Him in His word, the Bible, and through His Holy Spirit now in us.
2. The power or grace to change our lives to be more and more according to His will.
3. Provision for all our needs.
4. Everlasting life with God—If we die we shall be in His presence. We shall rise from the dead as Yeshua did (I Thessalonians 4:16,17, I Corinthians 15).
5. Incorporation into a new family of brothers and sisters who also have received His salvation. We now live lives of meaning and purpose.
6. The promise of the Holy Spirit is given to us. He indwells every believer.

We say Yeshua *fulfilled* the Hebrew Scriptures. This means several things. He *fulfilled* the law by loving perfectly according to the law. He *fulfilled* the prophecies of His death and resurrection. He replaced the temple system; He is now our priest and sacrifice to which the temple system pointed. He brought Israel's history to the height of its meaning, and taught the fullness of the older revelation.

By His death and resurrection Yeshua established a *New Covenant, a new agreement of a new means to be forgiven and empowered to live for God* (Jeremiah 31:31).

When we receive Yeshua, we are made part of His new people. A Jew is still part of his people Israel, and he is now part of the community of the followers of Yeshua. Just as God sought to make Israel a social and national witness to His Lordship by its reflection of His ways in its national life, so God has established New Covenant communities to express and live out the reality of new life in Yeshua. Our growth is encouraged and nurtured when we are part of the life of a congregation of Yeshua's followers. Furthermore, the reality of new life is demonstrated in our relationships with our brothers and sisters in the body of the Messiah.

We must understand the body of believers is God's means of carrying out His work in the world. By calling us Yeshua's body, God makes it clear we are organically part of Him and one another. To be cut off from regular participation in congregational life is to clearly be out of God's will and cut off from His blessing. Salvation in Yeshua is incorporation into a life together. A full discussion of the body of believers will be given in Chapter 5.

This section ends with a discussion of several important biblical terms: *repentance, faith, works, the flesh* and *lordship*.

Scripture calls on everyone who would receive God's salvation to *repent*. "Repent, for the kingdom of heaven is near." (Matthew 4:17). *Repentance* is a change in the way we think and a turning from our old ways to God's ways. Repentance is part of placing our trust in God—it is part of faith. Faith is not a way whereby we can be saved and yet do as we please. Faith is a trusting relationship with God that motivates our *obedience*.

This is why Yeshua warned in Matthew 7:21 that many

would say to Him, "Lord, Lord," in the day of judgment and He would say, "I never knew you. Away from me, you evil-doers!" Only the one who does the will of His Father is truly saved by faith, according to this passage.

We cannot receive Yeshua as Savior unless we receive Him as *Lord*, the Lord of our lives. If we so receive Him, we desire to verbally renounce and forsake everything in our lives that is not according to God's ways.

Scripture repeatedly teaches that a life of true faith produces true spiritual works (Ephesians 2:10). At the same time it teaches that *dead works* (Hebrews 6:11), which are produced by our human effort to attain righteousness before God, will fail. All efforts to attain righteousness without dependence upon God and empowerment from God are worthless. We cannot save ourselves by our *own works*.

Scripture calls all behavior motivated by self-effort, without the work of God's Spirit within us, *the flesh. The flesh* is man living by self, whether it produces sinful acts or seemingly good acts. The flesh profits nothing, but the Spirit gives life.

Now that you have truly received Yeshua, you have the wonderful privilege of living for Him. You can overcome the temptation to sin by confessing that you died to bondage to sin in Him (Romans 6:11).

> "I have been crucified with Messiah and I no longer live, but Messiah lives in me. The life I live in the body, I live by faith in the Son of God, who loved me and gave Himself for me." (Galatians 2:20)

You can have the power to do right and to pray for good things by confessing to Him daily that His resurrection power, even the Holy Spirit, is in you to enable you to accomplish all good things to which you are called. You know God. It is a wonderful life when we publicly repent and profess to enter new life in Him. Through this act we commit ourselves to the Messiah and to service in the body of His believers (Matthew 28:19, Acts 2:38,39).

You know Yeshua. Praise God for new life in Him. Man's purpose is to love God and enjoy Him forever.

STUDY QUESTIONS

1. How can we recognize the Messiah and the nature of His

   work? _____

   _____

2. _____ is the great chapter in
   the prophets describing the Messiah's death as a sacrifice
   and His resurrection.

3. The Scriptures teach the Messiah will come twice; the first

   time to _____

   and the second time to _____ .

4. Explain how Adam and Yeshua are representatives of the
   human race.

   a. Adam _____

   b. Yeshua _____

5. The New Covenant is _____

   _____

6. What are the three elements of God's salvation as seen in
   Yeshua?

   a. _____

   b. _____

   c. _____

7. List three important elements of being "in Him," "in
   Yeshua."

   a. _____

   b. _____

c. _____

8. Salvation is _____

_____

9. List some of the blessings of salvation described in this
   section.

_____

_____

_____

10. Repentance is _____

_____

11. Can one receive Yeshua as Savior without receiving Him as

    Lord? Explain: _____

_____

12. It is possible to be in God's will and not be part of a congrega-

    tion of believers? Explain: _____

_____

_____

_____

_____

VERSES FOR MEMORIZATION

Isaiah 9:6,7   Romans 10:9,10   John 3:16,17
Isaiah 53:6   Galatians 2:20

GOD AND THE MESSIAH

II. GOD AND THE MESSIAH

As we continue our study we will greatly expand the material in our first introductory chapter. As you begin this second study, it is our desire you will reinforce what you learned in the general introductory study and expand your knowledge and understanding of these topics.

SECTION A—THE EXISTENCE AND NATURE OF GOD

The Bible does not dwell on arguments to prove God's existence, but it is a mistake to assume it has nothing to say on the subject. The general drift of the Tenach is that God's existence is the natural and obvious conclusion for any reflective human being. Only the "fool says in his heart 'There is no God,' " (Psalm 14:1a).

For Israel, during her periods of faithfulness, to question the existence of God was unheard of. Of course He exists; He called our father Abraham, miraculously gave him a child through Sarah, supernaturally delivered us from Egypt, and enabled us to enter and control the Promised Land.

What about those nations who were not recipients of God's mighty acts of salvation and accompanying revelation? The answer might be that all peoples came from Noah and therefore had the knowledge of God and the flood, but their rebellion against God removed them from an intimate knowledge of Him. Romans chapters one and two give Scripture's primary teaching on this issue. Romans 1 begins with the declaration concerning all peoples that:

> ". . . since what may be known about God is plain to
> them, because God has made it plain to them. For
> since the creation of the world God's invisible qual-
> ities—His eternal power and divine nature—have
> been clearly seen, being understood from what has
> been made, so that men are without excuse." (Romans
> 1:19,20)

In other words, the existence of an intelligent creator God
is an obvious conclusion from the observation of the created
order; it is so obvious that it is more a conclusion from observing
creation than a conclusion of an argument. It is as plain as the
nose on your face.

Indeed, in looking at our own marvelous design, our hands,
our feet, our faces, and even more our spiritual abilities to love,
think, forgive, hate, be guilty, the obvious conclusion is, of
course, that God exists.

Only our age has produced such a widespread denial of the
reality of God. Men have concocted foolish theories of origins
without God and blinded others to the obvious senselessness of
their viewpoints. Why? The Apostle Paul said it is because the
old rebellion is still in the heart of man. He worships the creation instead of the creator. He may want to be his own lord or he
may create gods he can manipulate. Man does not want to face a
living Lord he cannot control. He suppresses the knowledge of
God and claims He does not exist. Romans 1:21,22, puts it like
this:

> "For although they knew God, they neither glorified
> Him as God nor gave thanks to Him, but their think-
> ing became futile and their foolish hearts were dark-
> ened. Although they claimed to be wise, they became
> fools. . . ."

The end result of this rebellion and its accompanying "dark-
ened mind" is all kinds of immorality, wickedness, covetous-
ness, malice, envy, murder, strife, and slander (Romans 1:29,30).
The Bible teaches man also has an inner moral sense by which
he knows he is under God's judgment. Man condemns others

for the very same sins he commits himself. Thus *by his own standard he is condemned.* In this state, every man and woman has the responsibility to seek the mercy of God!

In conclusion, we see the Bible teaches human beings are responsible before God because they are capable of knowing *He exists* and they stand under His judgment.

This knowledge of God is limited though. The fuller knowledge of what God is like is only obtained through the Bible. The Bible records God's works and words by which we can know His character.

In Genesis one, we see God is the creator who spoke the world into existence. The Psalmist captured this beautifully when he wrote:

"By the word of the Lord were the heavens made, their starry host by the breath of His mouth . . . for He spoke, and it came to be; He commanded, and it stood firm." (Psalm 33:6,9)

Only man among living creatures shares the developed speech capacity of God. He is created in God's image; his ability to create in a more limited way is related to his capacity to speak and visualize in his mind's eye. Words are our creative power. By confessing God's Word and praising Him in words, we change the whole direction of our lives. We go from failure and despair to triumph and joy.

As we continue to read in the Scriptures our picture of God is sharpened. From the Exodus we see that God is one who identifies with the outcast and the dispossessed. He rescued a nation of slaves. We also see God is sovereign, all knowing and all present.

In the revelation of God's law we see He is a God of the highest moral standards. He is clearly committed to truth, marital fidelity, business honesty, honoring parents, caring for the orphan and widow, justice in the courts, charity for the needy and care for the alien (or foreigner).

(Time should be taken here for the student to read Exodus 20-23 and Leviticus 19 to see the revelation of God's moral nature.)

As you read Exodus 20-23 and Leviticus 19 you notice God

often added these words to His most important moral and social instructions: "I am the Lord." God's very character stands behind His law and He will punish those who transgress it.

In the first lesson we saw that God is merciful and loving. He desires to forgive sin, iniquity and transgression (Exodus 34:6,7). However, He is also a fierce judge who will by no means excuse the guilty and unrepentant. Throughout the history of Israel we see both the great mercy and the severe judgment of God. God was merciful when Moses pleaded for His forgiveness after Israel fell into idolatry with the golden calf (Exodus 33:12ff). But God demands total allegiance, and severely judges those who cling to unrepented sin.

Jeremiah pleaded with King Zedekiah to repent and prevent the total destruction of Jerusalem by the Babylonians (Jeremiah 38:20-23). However, Zedekiah did not repent and Jerusalem was destroyed and his family put to death in severe judgment. God warned the people and their king, He desired to be merciful. However, when His warning went unheeded, His severe judgment befell them.

Samuel Schultz in the *Gospel of Moses*, notes this principle as a repeated aspect of God's revelation: God's offer of mercy always preceded judgment throughout Israel's repeated triumphs and tragedies.

God is both a loving Father and a severe Judge depending on where we stand with Him. We are called to love Him "with all our heart, soul, and strength" and to love "our neighbors as ourselves." (Mark 12, Deuteronomy 6:4ff).

Israel's history gives an extensive revelation of God, but it is not the fullest revelation of God. The fullest revelation of God is in Yeshua, the Messiah.

We are told in the Scriptures that God created man in His own image (Genesis 2:7). However, man is fallen and the reflection of God's image is marred.

Even so man is still more a reflection of God than all other creations (Gen. 1:26-28). Trees, animals, rivers, lakes, oceans, mountains, valleys, flowers, and fields do not reflect the nature of God to the extent human beings do, even though they are fallen. Only human beings clearly show forth the full range of moral qualities. Thus a perfect man would most clearly and fully reflect the nature and character of God. For us this is one of the roles of the Messiah, whose person is the topic of our next section.

STUDY QUESTIONS

1. Without biblical revelation, what are the two major truths about God that all peoples are capable of knowing?

   a. _____

   b. _____
2. What is the result of rebellion and the suppression of the

   knowledge of God? _____

   _____
3. Where can we turn to gain a more complete knowledge of the

   character of God? _____

   _____
4. Scripture shows God as both a loving Father and a stern Judge. However, in God's dealing with Israel and other peo-

   ples we see that God's _____

   always precedes _____ .

VERSES FOR MEMORIZATION
1. Romans 1:20
2. Review verses assigned in previous sections.

SECTION B—THE PERSON OF THE MESSIAH

In the Talmud, the great compendium of Jewish legal thought and discussion, we read of various things which pre-exist the creation of the world. God's wisdom and God's Torah (instruction) are said to pre-exist creation. The Talmud also states that in some sense the Messiah pre-exists the creation (Pes. 54 a Pesikta Rab 1526). In some way, the Messiah was part of God, uncreated. Yet we know the Messiah has an independent reality apart from God. Let's turn to the pages of the Tenach and see if we can clarify who the Messiah is and the nature of His person.

The first passage which speaks of redemption through the Messiah is Genesis 3:15. Immediately after the fall God gave the promise that the *seed of the woman* would give the mortal blow on the head to the serpent, the devil, but He would be bruised in the heel. By hindsight, knowing Yeshua was born physically from Miriam (Mary) but not Joseph, we understand why the passage says *the seed of woman*. This portion of Scripture begins what I call the seed promises of Scripture relating to the Messiah. Tracing these promises clarifies both the nature of the Messiah's person and work.

The seed promise is picked up again after the flood when, of the three children of Noah, Shem is given the special promise of God (Genesis 9:20). Shem was a forefather of Abraham who was called of God. Abraham was clearly the recipient of the Genesis 3:15 promise. In his seed, all of the nations of the earth were to be blessed.

The story of Abraham and Isaac is a wonderful pointer to the Messiah. Abraham and Sarah were beyond childbearing years. When Sarah was found to be barren, Abraham sought, *in the flesh*, to fulfill God's promise by his own efforts by having a child through Sarah's handmaid, Hagar. However, it was God's will to produce a child through the union of Abraham and Sarah. A miracle of rejuvenation enabled Abraham and Sarah to produce their only son, Isaac. Isaac is a prophetic image of the Messiah. These things should be noted about Isaac:

1. He was Abraham's *only son of miraculous birth*.
2. He was the *recipient of the seed promises* of Genesis 3:15

and Genesis 12:1-3.

3. He was *offered by his father* as a sacrifice.
4. And he *voluntarily accepted* the role of sacrifice and lay upon the altar.

Genesis 22 describes these amazing occurrences. The ancestor is tied to the descendant, as we explained before. In the Bible the ancestor often parallels in some way the life of his descendant in a prophetic way. Yeshua the Messiah is also the only son of miraculous birth of His Heavenly Father and the recipient of the seed promises. He was offered by His Father and voluntarily accepted the role of the sacrificial lamb.

The seed promise passed from Isaac to Jacob, not to his elder brother Esau. This was God's choice (Genesis 25:23). The stories of Esau selling his birthright and of Jacob stealing the blessing of Esau (Genesis 22), are emphasized because of their significance in regard to the seed promises. In Genesis 32:22ff, Jacob's name was changed after a special wrestling match with the Angel of God. We will return later to this passage.

Jacob's name is changed from Jacob (supplanter, grabber), to Israel (he who strives with God and prevails), and we see that his twelve sons will be the beginning of the nation. In a real sense, Israel as a nation shares the seed promises to bring blessing to the nations. However, one of the sons of Israel was singled out to be the father of Israel's kingly line. We read:

> "The scepter (the symbol of rule) will not depart from Judah, nor the ruler's staff from between his feet, until *He comes to whom it belongs* and the obedience of the nations is His." (Genesis 49:10)

He to whom it belongs is, in Hebrew, Shiloh. This might also be a name of the Messiah. Since the king is the representative of his people, the seed promise is especially connected to Israel's ultimate ruler. He will rule the nations. The *word "Messiah" means "anointed"* and refers to the anointing with oil given to kings and priests as a symbol of their anointing with the Spirit.

We do not read any further of these seed promises until we

come to II Samuel 7. The seed promise continues to be traced through David's line. His line will be the line of everlasting rulership and God will call his faithful successors, *His Son*. In Isaiah 9:6,7, we see this promise of an everlasting dynasty is to ultimately be fulfilled in one descendant.

> "For to us a child is born, to us a son is given, and the government will be on his shoulders. And he will be called Wonderful Counselor, Mighty God, Everlasting Father, Prince of Peace. Of the increase of his government and peace there will be no end. He will reign on David's throne and over his kingdom, establishing and upholding it with justice and righteousness from that time on and forever. The zeal of the Lord Almighty will accomplish this." (Isaiah 9:6,7)

Scripture clearly teaches there will be one supernatural Messiah King. His nature is described as more than human, it is divine. Other passages in the prophets further elaborate this picture.

In Isaiah 7:14 we read of a child who will be born of an *almah*. This Hebrew word is translated *virgin* because it refers to a young maiden of marriageable age, always presumed to be a virgin. Her son will be a sign to the House of David and a contrast to the wicked King Ahaz. His name will be Immanuel, God with us. This is a title or name similar to those in Isaiah 9:6.

In Micah 5:2 we read the Messiah, who is from ancient days, will be born in Bethlehem. In Zechariah 9:9 we read this king is *humble* and will enter Jerusalem upon a donkey. However, most amazing are the passages which speak of the "Messiah's suffering." Zechariah 12:10 speaks of Israel mourning for her pierced Messiah as one mourns for a son.

Psalm 22 was written by David. His own period of suffering and rejection was the occasion for a glimpse into the future in which his own descendant would die in crucifixion. The psalm ends with the promise that the nations of the world will remember this and turn to God through it. In Psalm 110:1 David called the Messiah his Lord,

> "The Lord says to my Lord: 'Sit at my right hand until

I make your enemies a footstool for your feet.' "

Isaiah 53 is the most amazing of all. This passage, fully described in the previous chapter, gives a vivid portrayal of the Messiah's death and resurrection.

Daniel 9:25-27 is a most remarkable passage. It predicts 69 weeks of years (483) from a decree until the cutting off (or death) of the Messiah. The decree is probably that of Artaxerxes in 445 B.C. After he is cut off, the Temple would be destroyed. This is historically amazing. The Messiah came at the predicted time, died, and the Temple was destroyed. So the seed promises clearly came to their fruition in a Messiah who died but came to life again.

The Tenach (Old Testament) spoke of the Messiah's supernatural divine nature. How can the Messiah be human and divine? How can He pre-exist creation and yet rule as a human son of David? These questions are resolved in a careful study of Scripture.

The Scripture gives us knowledge of the truth that God is what we call a uni-plural being. In Genesis 1:26 God says, "Let us make man in our image. . . ." Even the name for God, "Elohim," is a plural Hebrew form, with the plural masculine ending. Aspects of the mysterious uni-plural nature of God are found in those Scriptures which speak of a figure known as the Angel of the Lord. This figure is distinguished from God himself, yet he is called by the very holy covenant name of God.

This is the holy name of God which Jews refuse to pronounce so as not to take it in vain. In Genesis 18, three angels spoke with Abraham. We find in Genesis 18:10,17,20, that one angel is called by the holy name of God. He is God. In many English Bibles this is represented by writing LORD, in all capitals. In Genesis 32:24-31, Jacob wrestled with the Angel of the Lord. In verse 30 he recognized that it was no mere angel, for Scripture says,

"So Jacob called the place Peniel (Face of God) saying, "It is because I saw God face to face, and yet my life was spared."

In Exodus 3:2 we read the Angel of the Lord appeared to

Moses in the burning bush. However, in verse six we read God called to him from the bush and said, "I am the God of your father, the God of Abraham, the God of Isaac and the God of Jacob."

God told Moses He would send His angel before Israel. This angel is again called by the name of God.

This figure, the special Angel of God, is God in manifestation or revelation of Himself. He is not all of God, but is distinguished from God and yet is one with God.

In the New Covenant Scriptures we no longer read of this figure. There is an emphasis on the Holy Spirit, who is God, but distinguished from God as well. In the same way the Talmud speaks of *the Shekhinah, the divine glory and dwelling presence* of God. We find, also, that Yeshua has no earthly father, God is His Father.

Furthermore in John 8:58, Yeshua said, "before Abraham was I AM." Here He clearly identified Himself with the figure in Exodus three who, in verse 14, told Moses His name was "I AM." The Angel of God figure went into Yeshua, it is the component of His divine nature. Thus Yeshua is both fully human, a child of man through Miriam, and fully divine.

Other passages bring out the truth of the Messiah's divinity. In John 1:1 we read, "In the beginning was the *Word* and the *Word* was with God, and the *Word* was God."

God's Word, of course, is part of God. The Word is God's revelation, and of course, Yeshua is God's fullest revelation. The Word was in the beginning. In John 1:14 we read "The Word became flesh and lived for a while among us."

Colossians 2:9 says, "For in Messiah all the fullness of the Deity lives in bodily form." Philippians 2:6-11 is what many believe was an early hymn. Yeshua's pattern of giving up self is the exact opposite of Satan:

> "Who, being in very nature God (or who being the form of God), did not consider equality with God something to be grasped, but made Himself nothing, taking the very nature of a servant, being made in human likeness." (verses 6,7)

On the other hand, we must never forget Yeshua is fully man and was "tempted in every way, just as we are—yet was without sin." (Hebrews 2:17,18; 4:15)

Yeshua, being fully human and fully divine, perfectly fulfilled the mediation role foreshadowed by the high priest: "For there is one God and one mediator between God and men, the man, Messiah Yeshua." (I Timothy 2:5). He alone could enter the heavenly temple with the blood of His sacrifice so in Him we might enter into God's presence in prayer.

Yeshua's divinity is not an idolatrous teaching at all as some nonbelievers claim. Rather His divinity simply teaches that he is God in manifestation. It is perfectly within God's power and prerogative to manifest Himself in this way. Since man is created in God's image we are led to the conclusion that a manifestation in human form is the clearest revelation of God.

The divinity of Yeshua also leads us to the uni-plural nature of God. Yeshua is distinct from God as heavenly Father. He prays to God the Father, professes His great love for Him and submits Himself to the Father's will. The Angel of God passages teach this plurality as well. And Yeshua makes it clear that the Spirit of God is also divine.

(At this point the student should read John 15:26, 16:5-15.)

The Holy Spirit is one with God and yet distinct from the Father and Yeshua. The pre-existent Word, which became the Messiah's divine nature, was with God before creation. However, the person we know as Yeshua was a descendant of man through Miriam and came into existence as a human being in the first century.

God exists in plurality and unity. He is a community of three. The oneness of agreement and unity in this community of three is beyond our comprehension. It is beyond the oneness (ehad) of a man and wife in marriage (Genesis 2:24). This word *ehad*, used to describe the oneness of man and woman in marriage, is the same term used in Deuteronomy 6:4 where we read, "The Lord is one." It refers to a composite unity. In the composite unity of God there are three persons in an eternal community of love, oneness and agreement. This alone makes sense of the teaching that God is love.

"Agape" (or love) in the New Testament is selfless care for the other. If the eternal God before creation was absolutely singular ("Yachid" as later Jewish tradition since Maimonides has taught), then there could be no active love or self-giving in God before creation. Love is a relational term, a term expressing personal interaction. If love is an eternal part of God then self-giving among persons is part of the eternal reality of God. The creation of the world is not a selfish act, but the overflow of self-giving love. God's demand for our love is not selfish, but is His instruction for us to receive the same joy in giving ourselves in love to Him as He has in giving His love to us. He desires that we respond in love to His love.

All of Scripture and early Jewish writings reflect this uniplurality of God as the highest eternal level of reality. We praise God the Father for His revelation in Yeshua, the divine Messiah. His Spirit has set us free. These three yet-one are the eternal divine reality.

STUDY QUESTIONS

1. Genesis 3:15 teaches the Messiah would have his _____

_____ by Satan but that he would _____ of Satan.

2. What are four aspects of the sacrifice of Isaac which point to the later sacrifice of his descendant, the Messiah Yeshua?

a. _____

b. _____

c. _____

d. _____

3. In Scripture, there is a unique Angel of the Lord figure who appeared to Moses and wrestled with Jacob. What is unique about this figure?

_____

_____

4. Which of these statements expresses the truth of Scripture's teaching on Yeshua's nature?
   a. Yeshua was a human being in whom the Spirit dwelled.
   b. Yeshua was God yet appeared to be a man.
   c. Yeshua was both fully human and fully divine.
5. The word "ehad" in Scripture is often used to refer not to

   absolute singularity but what we have called a _____ .

VERSES FOR MEMORIZATION

John 1:1
Isaiah 7:14
Colossians 2:9

SECTION C—THE WORK OF THE MESSIAH

The Tenach points to the fact that the Messiah's work would consist of dying as a sacrifice for sin, rising from the dead, and eventually ruling over the whole earth on the throne of David. The New Testament greatly expands our understanding of the Messiah's wonderful work. The Scriptures teach that the Messiah came as fulfillment of the Tenach. The word "fulfillment" does not mean just to complete a prediction, nor does it mean to do away with. *It means to fulfill, to bring to reality the fullness of God's revelation and redemption.* Let's outline the meaning of the Messiah's fulfillment.

First of all, the Messiah fulfilled the teaching of the Old Testament Scriptures by being *a perfect example.* In His great compassion for the lost and wounded, we see the love of God. His life exemplified the height of Scripture's moral teaching. In Him there was no greed, only perfect self-giving. There was purity with no mixture of lust. He was just in all His ways, and completely honest. He loved God with all His heart, soul, strength, and might, and loved His neighbor as Himself.

We get a glimpse of the divine in Yeshua's tender patience for children, His compassion for sinners, and His healing power applied to the sick. However, we also see His love expressed in holy anger at religious hypocrites, the proud and perverted self-seekers. The Gospel of Matthew presents Yeshua as *living Torah.* It is in this light Peter said, "To this you were called, because Messiah suffered for you, leaving you an example, that you should follow in His steps." (I Peter 2:21).

Yeshua also brought the Tenach to its fullness by His *teaching.* He was its greatest interpreter. This is brought out most vividly by the Sermon on the Mount in Matthew chapters five through seven and His parables in such chapters as Matthew 13 and 25, Luke 15 and 16.

(It is a good idea for the student to read these chapters at this time.)

In Matthew, chapter five through seven we see those characteristics of holiness which should mark the lives of all Yeshua's followers. First, Yeshua outlined those moral qualities which lead to comfort and joy in God's kingdom. They include meekness, humility, hungering and thirsting for true righteousness, and poverty of spirit. This last quality is a genuine recognition of our own lack of self-righteousness and our need to receive in spirit from God.

After this Yeshua explained the law showing how all transgression of God's moral law is first preceded by an evil heart. We must look at what the Torah says to our hearts. We may not have murdered, but if we have hate in our hearts, we have the seed and evil of murder in us. It is the same with lust and adultery. Yeshua brought out the truth that Torah leads us, when rightly understood, to the standard of love and compassion even for our enemies. By His teaching, the standards of God are intensified.

No one can read Matthew five without seeing how distant we are from God's ways. We must depend upon God's grace and mercy. Yeshua said He "did not come to abolish the Law . . . but to fulfill it," that "not the smallest letter, nor the least stroke of a pen, will by any means disappear from the Law until everything is accomplished." Relaxing the law makes one "least in the kingdom." Softening the law takes away the knowledge whereby man sees his need of cleansing and forgiveness.

Then in Matthew six Yeshua taught on prayer, charity, and fasting. Verses 25-33 gives the most amazing teaching on God's fatherly love for us. We are not to be anxious about material needs, for our heavenly Father who clothes the lilies of the field and provides for the birds of the air will much more take care of His faithful. Yeshua concluded, "But seek first His kingdom and His righteousness, and all these things will be given to you as well. Therefore do not worry. . . ."

Yeshua also fulfilled the predictive aspects of the Tenach. These include specific predictions of the place of His birth and of His death and resurrection. But there is much more. Yeshua is the representative head of Israel and of the whole human race, since Israel is the representative of the nations.

Yeshua's life parallels the life of the nation. He went to Egypt to avoid death, He went through the waters of baptism (parallel to Israel passing through the sea), the Spirit of God came on him (parallel to Israel's being under the cloud) (I Corinthians 10), and was tempted in the wilderness for 40 days (parallel to Israel's test for 40 years wandering in the wilderness). (See Matthew two through four.)

But in contrast to Israel, Yeshua perfectly overcame in each test. Therefore *in Him* Israel can be considered as having passed the test, and in Him, will fulfill its role. Yeshua brought to fullness the life and history of the nation.

In addition, Yeshua brought new meaning to the feasts of Israel. He is the Passover Lamb for us. In Him we enter Sabbath rest (Hebrews 4 and John 5) and live in the peace of God. He is the light of the world proclaimed in the Feast of Sukkoth (dwelling in tents to recall Israel's life on the desert when God met all Israel's needs). In Him all our needs are met. The harvest celebration of Shavuoth or Pentecost is the harvest of the righteous in which we are given the Spirit (Acts 2) and many are gathered into the Kingdom. In Yom Kippur we see He is our atonement, our high priest and sacrifice. The meaning of all the special Jewish days is enhanced by Him.

Yeshua also replaced the temple system with the new priesthood. This is why when He died the curtain of the Temple was torn in two (Matthew 22:51). This curtain separated the holy place from the most holy place (Holy of Holies) in the Temple. In the most holy place God maintained a special presence of Himself. Only the high priest could enter the Holy of Holies once a year on Yom Kippur with the blood of Atonement.

Everyone could see through the temple system that they were separated from God and had to enter God's holiest presence indirectly through the priest. But Yeshua is the true high priest who entered the Holy of Holies of heaven. He brought the blood of His own sacrifice. He is now forever at the right hand of God. Therefore, we can, in Him, enter into the very Holy of Holies of heaven. The earthly curtain of separation was torn to show in Yeshua we all may enter into the holiest heavenly presence of God. (These truths are especially taught in Hebrews four through nine.)

This is why we are told to pray to the Father in the Name of Yeshua (John 14:13). The New Testament model of prayer shows us to address our prayer to God the Father. We come in the Name of Yeshua because in Him alone we have the privilege and right to come before our Heavenly Father. We are righteous in Him. (Illustration: I have a brother-in-law whose cousin owns a baseball team. After visiting his city and attending a game, we were privileged to enter the private lounge where the owners, managers, and other prominent people gathered. I was able to enter because I was given a pass with the name of the owner. I had no authority of my own, but could enter in the owner's name.)

This leads us to take a look at the work of Yeshua under the headings: sacrifice, high priest and king.

First of all, Yeshua is our sacrifice. This has many wonderful meanings. Sacrifice implies *laying down your life in love for another*. Yeshua laid down His life in the greatest demonstration of love for us (Romans 5:6-8). The fullest demonstration of love is when someone who is righteous gives up his life to save someone who is unrighteous. Parents give their lives for children who are at times unworthy. Heroes give up their lives for others as well. When such an act of love occurs, the rescued party is usually transformed. His life was spared while a more worthy person's life was sacrificed. It is just such an outpouring of love we see in Yeshua.

Yeshua as sacrifice is also our representative. We are in Him by faith. He died in our place and we are considered to have died in Him. Romans 5:8 says, "But God demonstrates His own love for us in this: While we were still sinners, Messiah died for us."

Yeshua is also the representative of the Father; in Him we see the Father's suffering love. Yeshua is the Father's gift of love and He suffered to see His Son tortured for us. God suffers and mourns over the sins of the human race; He feels our pain and desires our good. This is seen in Yeshua's sacrifice.

Yeshua's sacrifice is also a revelation of good and evil. True good is full of love, it seeks the benefit of others. The forfeiture of life when it will produce greater good for others is the nature of love. Yeshua went through utter agony not only in being crucified but in bearing the sin of the world and being separated from the Father. No one can fathom the depth of His anguish.

Yeshua's sacrifice revealed the true nature of our evil. Selfishness and pride of position caused our ancient leaders to turn over the only perfectly good man to be put to death. The same selfishness motivated the Romans to crucify Him. Men do not want the exposure which the presence of goodness brings. Their response is "crucify Him." We are part of this sin, because our sins put Him there, the whole human race was *represented* in His rejection. But His death is my sacrifice and if I by faith admit I deserved the death He died, and that I am a sinner, but *identify* with His death for me, then I am free.

Yeshua died in my place so I would not come into judgment. His act of sacrifice awakens me to repentance. His love moves me to seek God's forgiveness and I become a "new creation in Messiah." II Corinthians 5:17 says, "Therefore, if anyone is in Messiah, he is a new creation; the old has gone, the new has come!"

Yeshua is also my *priest*. Not only did He enter into the heavenly temple with the blood of His sacrifice, but He now is continually interceding on my behalf.

Hebrews says, "Therefore He is able to save completely those who come to God through Him, because He always lives to intercede for them" (7:25). Yeshua lifts those prayers up before God which are led of the Spirit. By His priestly work, because I am in Him, I am *spiritually* able to be present at the heavenly throne of God in prayer.

(We encourage the student to set aside a time to read the marvelous book of Hebrews which describes Yeshua's work.)

The resurrection is the capstone of Yeshua's work. It was not possible for death to hold Him. The third day he rose from the dead. The evidence, historically, for Yeshua's resurrection is His victory over death. By it He is seen as Lord and *King*. Furthermore, we not only died in Him, but rose in Him.

> "If we have been united with Him in His death, we will certainly also be united with Him in His resurrection." (Romans 6:5)

This truth teaches several things. First, *when Yeshua returns, we shall be raised from the dead and will be given a spiritual body* like His which is not limited as our present bodies (I Thessalonians 4:16). His resurrection gives us assurance of our own everlasting life in Him. If we die before His return, we shall spiritually be in God's presence until we are given our new bodies.

Because we are in Him, *there is also the present reality of resurrection life in us.* We are spiritually alive to God, have substantial healing for our bodies, and victory over sin in Him. We are able to conquer sins such as selfishness, anger, hate, lust, and worry in Him.

A crucial biblical truth is that the death and resurrection of Yeshua is not just an historic fact or promise of a future event; it is something to be experienced as a present power in our lives. Romans six is a great chapter on this truth. It says:

> "Don't you know that all of us who were baptized into Messiah Yeshua were baptized into His death? We were therefore buried with Him through baptism into death in order that, just as Messiah was raised from the dead through the glory of the Father, we too may live a new life. . . . In the same way, count your- selves dead to sin but alive to God in Messiah Yeshua." (vv 6:3,4,11)

In spiritual identity with Yeshua (as pictured in baptism), we have spiritually died and have spiritually been raised from the dead. This is the doctrine of our co-death and resurrection. The Scripture teaches we have been given a new born-again spirit and power to no longer yield to our old sin nature (we have died to our old nature). We can now live out our new nature. When we are tempted, we can immediately think of Yeshua's death and resurrection and say:

> "I died in Him to sin and I have His resurrection power to live a new life in love. I overcome this temp- tation and place my mind on Him and turn my atten- tion now to praise and His service."

(The student should repeat this after the teacher.)

When a believer does this, he actually draws from the power of Yeshua's death and resurrection and becomes an overcomer. This power overcomes anger, lust, hate, and greed. If you have never understood this, why not take God's provision by faith right now? Thank Him that you died in Messiah and are raised to new life in Him. Live from now on in His power.

STUDY QUESTIONS

1. Describe the New Testament meaning of the word "fulfill."

_____

_____

_____

2. In Yeshua's teaching, all transgression of God's moral law is

   preceded by _____

_____

_____

3. What is the significance of the tearing of the Temple curtain?

_____

_____

_____

4. Yeshua's sacrifice has several prominent elements. Name three primary elements of His sacrifice.

   a. _____

   _____

   b. _____

   c. _____

VERSES FOR MEMORIZATION
Romans 5:8   Matthew 6:53   Romans 6:11   II Corinthians 5:17

THE CALL TO HOLY LIVING

III. THE CALL TO HOLY LIVING

In this chapter, we want to outline some central aspects of the new lifestyle to which we are called in the Messiah. The student should clearly understand these important areas of truth: the nature of repentance, renunciation and restitution; victory over the devil; separation from the world; the power of the Word; and the fruit of the Spirit. *The word "holy" means separate. We are called to be separated from the ways of the world and separated unto the ways of God.*

SECTION A—THE WORLD, THE FLESH, AND THE DEVIL

Problems in the life of the believer stem from three intertwined, interrelated areas: the world, the flesh, and the devil. The word "world" does not refer to the value of people or to the beauties of God's creation. Of "world" in this latter sense, we read, "For God so loved the world" (John 3:16). *The word "world" in its negative sense refers to the present world system of evil under the control of Satan.*

The world system is based on selfishness and greed; it is characterized by a hedonistic "me-first" philosophy. To give one's self to selfishness and that which demeans the beauty of God's purposes and standard is to become worldly. The way of the world is seen all around us from 42nd Street palaces of lust to corporate greed, from loose talk to keeping up with the Joneses as a motivation. In John it says:

"Do not love the world or anything in the world. If anyone loves the world, the love of the Father is not in him. For everything in the world—the cravings of

sinful man, the lust of his eyes and the boasting of
what he has and does—comes not from the Father but
from the world. The world and its desires pass away,
but the man who does the will of God lives forever."
(2:15-17)

Believers are motivated by love for God and other people.
They love not the things of the world: wealth, pride of position,
power, and selfish pleasures. It is love and service which bring
joy.

The flesh is a second major problem area in the believer's
life. *The flesh is "the old man," or the person activated by the
old selfish nature.* Flesh does not refer to our physical body
created by God. But our physical body and its desires are one
source of fleshly temptation. Other sources are pride, anger,
insecurity, fear, and hate. *The flesh includes the totality of
sinful patterns developed in our old life.*

Paul wrote that nothing good dwelt in his flesh (Romans
7:8). Each person carries with him his own unique organization
of sinful patterns, desires, and weaknesses. For one person the
flesh tends to gluttony and drunkenness, in another to loss of
temper, in another to adultery, pride, and laziness. Every person has some degree of all these tendencies in his flesh, but in
different proportions and strengths. We are all alike yet all
unique as sinners. Our flesh is weak and tempts us to evil, but
we must learn to overcome it. It is incited to evil by the entice-
ments of the world system.

Thirdly, there is the devil. The devil and his hosts of de-
mons try to bring believers into bondage by implanting ideas in
their minds, and intensifying, through their spiritual powers,
the temptations of the world. Those who have been involved in
demonic idolatrous practices forbidden in Scripture often are
very weak before the power of the devil. These practices
include: astrology, magic (black and white), witchcraft, divination, Ouija boards, card reading, palmistry, water witching,
some forms of hypnotism, crystal ball gazing, and a host of other
occult practices.

Gross sexual immorality often brings oppression. The
mature believer can discern the presence of powerful demonic

spirits of lust in the lewd entertainment centers of many cities. Continued bitterness and unforgiveness also bring oppression. And these sins take a toll on following generations. The Bible does give us clear directions on overcoming the power of the devil, though.

The interrelation of the world, the flesh and the devil is clear. Satan and his hosts tempt us through the enticement of the world which appeals to our flesh. When we succumb to temptations, especially in a repeated way, we give up spiritual ground to Satan and come under demonic bondage or oppression. But Scripture gives us ways to overcome the world, the flesh, and the devil.

The first approach to overcoming in any area is repentance. *Repentance is a conscious turning from sin; we agree with God that we have sinned, are genuinely sorry for our sin, and make a clear decision by the power of God to turn from it.* Central in this process is confession to God and asking His forgiveness. It is good to *renounce the sin* and verbally say, "I take back from Satan any ground I have given in the Name of Yeshua and command all the hosts of evil to be gone from me."

Renunciation, if genuine, leads to *restitution*, that is, the making right of any sin against another, whether it is financial restitution or a personal apology.

Let us now look at how to more specifically overcome the world and the flesh. The power of the flesh is broken by confessing our co-death and resurrection with the Messiah and maintaining a constant attitude of praise and thanksgiving. Whether it be pride or anger or lust, it is good to confess a prayer composed from Scripture.

Confessing or quoting the Word of God against temptation is powerful. It dispels the powers of Satan. This was shown by the example of Yeshua who quoted Scripture against every temptation of Satan. Here is a general Scriptural confession to overcome the world. You can use prayer, composed from Romans chapter six, or compose one of your own:

"I have died to my old flesh nature in the Messiah Yeshua, and I have risen from the dead to new life in Him. I have power in Yeshua to overcome this sin and purpose now to give myself to thoughts and involvements for God's Kingdom."

Or quote a passage such as Galatians 2:20, which says:

"I have been crucified with Messiah and I no longer live, but Messiah lives in me. The life I live in the body, I live by faith in the Son of God, who loved me and gave Himself for me."

There are Scriptures which relate to particular sins and it is good to learn such passages for "besetting sins," that is, sins which are repeated and hard to break. A true desire to live a godly life is only fulfilled if we give ourselves to the discipline of replacing ungodly habits with godly ones. Scripture teaches there are two steps to restructuring our behavior. *First, we must put off ungodly behavior and stop sinning, and secondly, cultivate a new righteous behavior, which is the opposite of the old.*

"You were taught, with regard to your former way of life, to put off your old self, which is being corrupted by its deceitful desires; to be made new in the attitude of your minds; and to put on the new self, created to be like God in true righteousness and holiness." (Ephesians 4:22-24) "Depart from evil and do good. (Ps. 34)

After this general prescription for overcoming sin, Paul gave specific instruction for specific problems [Ephesians 4:25-32].

The liar must begin a program of telling the truth. The thief is cured when he gets honest work and gives to others out of his profit. The greedy person must begin a program of regular generosity in the power of Yeshua, then he will be changed. Bitterness, rage, anger, and slander must be replaced by thoughts of others' needs, and by the compassion and forgiveness of Yeshua even for enemies. Only then do we *act* in love toward others.

Satan's deception often appeals to our pride, causing us to think we are stronger than we are. It is crucial to walk in the Spirit in such a way that we do not place ourselves in positions of unnecessary temptation from the world. Scripture says, "flee youthful lusts."

Often a more mature believer, counselor, or elder, can help you develop a program for change. Be humble and open to such help. *Pride will thwart growth in all areas.*

Satan's hosts also are involved in our temptations. Although he has been defeated by Yeshua, God allows Satan to test us. (Ephesians 6:10ff). This is for our strengthening if we properly resist. "Resist the devil, and he will flee from you." (James 4:7).

Satan's hosts try to inject negative and sinful thoughts into our minds (Ephesians 6:16, 2 Corinthians 10:5). If we succumb to temptation repeatedly we come under an oppression of the devil and are continually overwhelmed in that particular area. These may be areas of sexual lust, pride, anger, gluttony, or uncontrollable buying. How does one walk in victory over the devil? This is our present concern.

DELIVERANCE FROM THE POWER OF THE DEVIL

There is a raging but foolish debate over whether or not a believer can be possessed by the devil. As with many such debates this is a needless debate. Any believer belongs to God, and of course cannot be possessed by the devil. The Bible does not talk about possession, only about being demonized. To even ask whether a person has a demon within or is oppressed from without illustrates the problem, for the devil's oppression is non-spatial, in the realm of the Spirit. Just as the old flesh still exists to test us, so Satan is still present to use his power in oppressing us through the flesh. But it is every believer's birthright to be free from satanic oppression. Here are steps to freedom:

Step # 1: Thorough Housecleaning and Deliverance
Many Jewish people today have strayed from the ways of

the Torah. Either they or their ancestors have engaged in occult
practices or gross immorality which has produced oppression
by the devil. Everyone should make a thorough inventory of his
life, according to Scriptural injunctions to "examine ourselves"
(I Corinthians 10:28) and "judge ourselves" (I Corinthians
10:31), so he will not be judged. Many have felt real release in
confession and renunciation.

We may be ignorant of an ancestor's involvement and it is
well to renounce all these things, especially areas of direct
involvement. Command Satan to flee and command his hold to
be broken in these areas. Deuteronomy 15:9-12 begins by listing
occult practices. Here is a prayer inventory which begins there:

"Heavenly Father, I come to You now in the
Name of Yeshua. I thank You and praise You that
You have saved me. I desire to be clean and pure
before You, to serve You in love. Therefore I have
come to confess and renounce all relationship with
occult involvements and serious sins which bring
oppression. I claim freedom from oppression in these
areas and take back any ground given to Satan
through connection with these sins.

"I break in Yeshua's Name any bondage to ances-
tral connections or curses from these involvements. I
confess and renounce all occult involvement, including: astrology, palmistry, crystal ball gazing, card laying, witchcraft, pendulum divination, tea leaf reading, ESP, hypnosis, spiritism, magic (both black and
white), water witching, the Ouija board, and all other
occult arts.

"Furthermore, I confess and renounce all involvement with illicit drugs, drunkenness and Eastern meditations and abilities. I renounce involvement in any Eastern or pagan religions. I renounce
mind control and transcendental meditation.

"I confess all immorality, adultery, homosexual-
ity, fornication, and other sexual sins. I purpose to
forgive all, my parents and others who come to mind,
who may have caused me harm. (Take time to specif-

ically name anyone or anything you can think of.) In addition, I promise to ask forgiveness and right the wrongs I have committed against others wherever possible.

"I break the bondage of the kingdom of Satan now. I am Yours, Lord. I pray to love You with all my heart, soul, strength, and might. Praise You, Lord, in Yeshua's Name, Amen."

Take some time at this point to praise God. Satan flees at the presence of praise.

Step #2: Deliverance Teamwork

If there are any particular areas where you do not have victory, perhaps a prayer team which can also command your release is the solution. The gift of discernment is helpful here. (The student should seek counsel before launching into deliverance. The problem may be one of the flesh.)

If we do not learn to overcome the flesh, we cannot maintain victory over the devil. A wise counselor or elder can often discern if a specific prayer deliverance session is necessary. Fasting and prayer break Satan's power (Mark 9:29). Every person should know as a believer he has authority over the demonic hosts in the Name of Yeshua and can free himself in Yeshua's Name. But the humility to seek help when unsuccessful is part of the battle and half of the victory.

Step #3: Putting on the Armor of God

Ephesians 6:10ff is a great passage which gives direction for walking in freedom from the devil's oppression. It says:

"Finally, be strong in the Lord and in His mighty power. Put on the full armor of God so that you can take your stand against the devil's schemes. For our struggle is not against flesh and blood, but against the rulers, against the authorities, against the powers of this dark world and against the spiritual forces of evil in the heavenly realms. Therefore, put on the full

armor of God so that when the day of evil comes, you
may be able to stand your ground."

The spiritual armor is described in this chapter. It is an
analogy from ancient military armor. This is the description:

1. The Belt of Truth—Standing firmly for truth and speaking the truth in love strengthens us. We stand on the
   truth of God's Word, the Bible.
2. The Breastplate of Righteousness—Living a righteous
   life based on our righteousness in Him protects us from
   wounds to our heart.
3. Feet Shod with the Gospel of Peace—We are engaged not
   in idleness or laziness but in action, walking and moving
   to spread the gospel to those who do not yet believe.
   Involvement in witness is a protection. Laziness here
   opens us to attack.
4. Shield of Faith—This is to extinguish the flaming arrows
   of the evil one. Faith is standing on God's Word; faith is
   an active trust in God and His promises so Satan's
   arrows of fear, discouragement, and worry do not pene-
   trate us.
5. The Helmet of Salvation—We protect our minds by fo-
   cusing on and living in the truth of our constant salvation in Him.
6. The Sword of the Spirit, which is the Word of God—We
   use the sword of the Spirit to attack the devil; quoting
   Scripture against the devil's attacks wounds him and
   causes him to flee.

We are enjoined to pray in the Spirit, praising, and making
our requests known to God. Victory over the world, the flesh
and the devil is a product of a life of praise, a life filled with the
Spirit, and a life lived in the power of the Word. These topics
will be dealt with in our next sections.

VERSES FOR MEMORIZATION

I John 2:15,16   Galatians 2:20   James 4:7

STUDY QUESTIONS

1. What does the word "world" refer to? _____

_____

2. What does the word "flesh" refer to? _____

_____

3. List those behaviors which are a part of repentance:

    a. _____

    b. _____

    c. _____

    d. _____

4. The two steps to overcoming fleshly behavior and restructuring our lives taught in Ephesians four, are:

    a. _____

    b. _____

5. List and briefly define the three steps of freedom from the devil.

    a. _____

    _____

    b. _____

    _____

    c. _____

_____

SECTION B—THE SPIRIT AND THE WORD

We have seen many people freed from the world, the flesh and the devil. Incurable schizophrenics, psychotics, and the depressed have been miraculously freed using the steps listed in Section A. This has occurred even when psychiatrists had said there was no hope. Continuing to walk in freedom and joy is related to living by the Word in the power of the Spirit.

In this way lives are transformed. Failures became successes, and the depressed become joyful, the neurotic become calm and confident. Let's turn to the Bible's teaching on the *Ruach ha Kodesh* (the Holy Spirit) to begin our study on the Spirit and the Word.

The *Holy Spirit is the Person of God sent by Yeshua to be our permanent companion.* He is present with us at all times. Because of this, Yeshua said it was expedient that He go away because His presence upon earth was limited physically. The Holy Spirit is not limited physically. He is *omnipresent, present everywhere* (John 15 and 16).

The Holy Spirit is the present power of God in us. John the Baptist promised the Messiah would baptize (immerse) in the Holy Spirit (Matthew 3:11). Joel 2:28-30 described the future outpouring of God's Spirit on all believers. It says it would be accompanied by prophetic powers, visions, and dreams, which accompany the presence of the Spirit. *In the Old Testament period*, only special people, *prophets, kings, and priests*, were given this *anointing*, But in the New Covenant period *every believer* can have this anointing. Ezekiel 36 promised God would place His Spirit in us as part of the New Covenant.

In Acts 2:1ff, we read about the outpouring of the Holy Spirit on the believers in Yeshua, as described in Joel. This outpouring was accompanied by great miracles of speaking in tongues. The 120 followers of Yeshua were by the Spirit able to speak in languages they had never learned. They spoke the gospel (the Good News) to Jews from many countries in the languages of their lands. This supernatural sign of the Spirit accompanied the filling of the Spirit on other occasions as well (Acts 8:17, 10:46, 19:6).

Messianic Jews are spiritually united with all true Christian followers of Yeshua. They are rooted in the biblical Jewish heritage but also draw from the wisdom of the church. Unfortunately, some Jews get caught up in needless debates of the church. In this century, the believing church is divided over the Holy Spirit. Some people believe the baptism in the Holy Spirit takes place when a person is born again. They also believe the supernatural gifts of the Spirit were only to establish the first century church and are no longer given by the Spirit.

Others believe the baptism of the Spirit is distinct from the salvation experience and must be sought independently of it. They may think that without speaking in tongues a person does not have this experience. They believe that all of the supernatural gifts of the Spirit are valid today (see list in I Corinthians 12, I Peter 4 and Romans 12, e.g., tongues, prophecy, healing, miracles). We thank God for those who rediscovered, and by faith, received the power of the Spirit but the issues of this debate have been unnecessarily divisive.

When we look at the 19th century and examine the teachings of great saints of the church in that era, we sometimes find a broader view of the Holy Spirit. Charles Finney, R.A. Torrey, and D.L. Moody, for example, all believed in the gifts of the Spirit and later anointings of power in the Spirit. They experienced supernatural gifts but did not make any one gift the test of spiritual life. We mention this to warn you of the controversy which exists and to encourage you to avoid division.

The *baptism of the Spirit* is the positional possession of every believer at the time he is born again. We are in Yeshua; He was filled with the Spirit and in Him we have His blessings. We have died with Him, been raised with Him, and been made partakers of the Spirit in Him. We are healed in Him.

All of us should therefore experience the Spirit as a living reality in our lives.

> "You, however, are controlled not by the sinful nature but by the Spirit, if the Spirit of God lives in you. And if anyone does not have the Spirit of Messiah, he does not belong to Messiah . . . the Spirit Himself testifies with our spirit that we are God's children." (Romans 8:9,16)

However, not all believers *experience* the reality of the Spirit. They have not by faith taken this reality into their lives. We call this taking of the reality, appropriation.

It is as if someone deposited $1,000 into your checking account. It is really yours. You have it. But until you write a check on it or withdraw some of it you do not experience the reality of it in your life. *Positionally you have the money, but practically you have not appropriated it or taken it.* It is the same with the Holy Spirit; positionally He is ours, but practically we have not drawn on His reality. *Many use the phrase, "baptism in the Spirit" to refer to the position; they debate with those who use the term to describe the first experience of one's coming into the practical reality.* Let's not debate: let's enter into the reality.

Ephesians 5:18 commands us to "be filled with the Spirit." The Holy Spirit is the down payment on our final and total redemption in the day of resurrection. He is the guarantee of our future inheritance in the future Kingdom. Let's be filled with Him.

The *practical* experience of the baptism of the Spirit comes by faith. First we tell God we desire to walk in the fullness of the Spirit, we have confessed all known sin, and ask to experience this blessing. Then we confess the word of promise that the Father gives the Spirit to those who ask, praying until we have the assurance of it (Luke 11:13).

The experience of the baptism in the Spirit is unique for each person. For many people there is just an inner sense of conviction and new power for living and witnessing. Some are literally knocked off their feet. Internally there is a new intuitive experience of the Spirit's promptings and direction.

The *laying on of hands* in prayer is helpful for many since the faith of others strengthens one's faith to receive the gift, but it is often received without the *laying on of hands*, too (Acts 2, 10:46). This, of course, is true of healing as well. A great many today who receive the practical reality of this baptism speak in tongues. This is because there is much teaching on this and many thus have the faith to receive this gift. Some believe that tongues is the sign of the reception of the Baptism in the Spirit.

Should you *speak in tongues?* Speaking in tongues is a faith expression. It is in most cases not a recognizable human language as in Acts chapter two. Some have more developed verbal abilities than others. *This gift expresses submission to God, praise in the Spirit, and prayer for things for which we know not how to pray. The exercise of it increases our spiritual sensitivity.* But there have been men of God who have had discernment, healing, and miracles operating through them, and yet have never spoken in tongues. My advice is, why not ask God for it? Open your mouth in faith and speak. If you do not receive the gift of tongues, do not become preoccupied with it.

Any unwillingness to receive this "least of gifts" (I Corinthians 14) may be a point of contention between you and God. Pride may be the root of your unwillingness, because you don't want to seem foolish. How many are the humorous stories of those who even spoke against the gift and were supernaturally given it! We encourage you to be open to God's leading on this gift. We have found a significant difference in growth in both individuals and groups who are open to the Holy Spirit and all of His legitimate Biblical manifestations.

The power of the Spirit is cultivated by daily renewing our submission to Him in prayer. We thus are filled with the Spirit constantly, and this power is cultivated as we sensitively obey our conscience. Our conscience is sensitized and made a more accurate guide through the reading and memorization of the Word. As we grow we can more intuitively sense the Holy Spirit speaking to us. He guides us and gives us a sense of freedom to proceed, stop, or change directions. He also gives supernatural insight at times when situations require His help.

But we can misinterpret the Spirit's leading and the sense of yes or no that comes from Him. Even so, God is still Lord and will protect us. As long as we test the leading of the Spirit to make sure it is according to the Bible, we cannot get too far off track. *Word and Spirit go together. The Word must always be the objective test of the Spirit (I John 4:1). Nothing contrary to the written Word is ever of God.*

As we cultivate praise and thanksgiving in all situations because we know God is in control, the Spirit fills our life. God "inhabits the praises of" His people (Ps. 22:3). Praising God in all circumstances is commanded in Scripture and is an act of faith.

We are to rejoice in the Lord always (Philippians 4:4-8). We can do this because God has promised "All things God works for the good of those who love Him, who have been called according to His purpose." (Romans 8:28). God raised Yeshua from the dead, we can believe Him.

We wish to close our teaching on the Holy Spirit by turning to the teaching of Galatians 5:16 which says, "So I say, live by the Spirit, and you will not gratify the desires of the sinful nature" (the flesh).

To live by the flesh is to walk according to its promptings, temptations, and pride. To live by the Spirit is to depend on His leading and power for all we do. We may undertake projects which seem good, but actually are dead works. We are neither led of the Spirit nor empowered of the Spirit for these endeavors. This leads to failure even though there may appear to be some success on a shallow level. Whatever is not built by prayer and the Spirit is of no worth.

To walk in the flesh is to walk by mere human ideas and desires, whether they are grossly sinful or seemingly good. To walk by the Spirit is to walk in faith, prayer, and the Spirit's leading and power. Many believers are weak because they do not desire above all else to be *truly* spiritual. They have never learned this primary lesson. They neither have the insight nor the power of a truly spiritual person.

What does it mean to be spiritual? It means having the ability to sense the Spirit's leading and be empowered to walk in His ways as we live by God's love. It is living by our spirit's intuitive communication with God's Spirit as based on the Word.

Walking in the flesh eventually produces the works of the flesh. They are listed in Galatians 5:19ff and are contrary to the Spirit. They are:

". . . sexual immorality, impurity and debauchery, idolatry and witchcraft; hatred, discord, jealousy, fits of rage, selfish ambition, dissensions, factions and envy; drunkenness, orgies, and the like. I warn you, as I did before, that those who live like this will not inherit the kingdom of God."

To practice life in the flesh is to be an unbeliever, for no matter what such a person may say with his mouth, he is a hypocrite. However, when a person is spiritual, as we have defined it, the fruit of the Spirit is produced in his life. Fruit takes time to grow, it requires pruning for its growth. *Scripture is absolutely clear that the fruit of the Spirit provides us with the true test of whether or not we are spiritual.* The gifts of the Spirit are not the tests of spirituality. They are tools by which the carnal (fleshly) may possess but choose not to grow.

> "The fruit of the Spirit is love, joy, peace, patience, kindness, goodness, faithfulness, gentleness and self-control. Against such things there is no law. Those who belong to Messiah Yeshua have crucified the sinful nature with its passions and desires. Since we live by the Spirit, let us keep in step with the Spirit." (Galatians 5:22-25)

Read over this list of qualities; perhaps compare it with the qualities listed in Matthew 5:1ff. Depend on the Spirit daily to produce this fruit in you. In dependence on God pray them into your life. Indeed, try to act in ways consistent with these qualities. *Love and joy are produced as we identify with and receive the Messiah's love.* As He is gentle we can be gentle. So also with kindness and goodness—they are produced by the Messiah's love in us. Patience comes through responding to trying situations by faith, quoting the Word's answer to our difficulties.

Friends, our deepest desire for you is that you be spiritual. Then you will have joy and peace! You will see people and situations with insight and understanding you never dreamed of. May God make the prayer of your heart to love Him with your all and thereby be spiritual. Make this your first request of every day.

STUDY QUESTIONS

1. In regard to our study of the *Ruach ha Kodesh* or Holy Spirit,
   define the contrast between the Old Testament period and
   the New Covenant age.

   _____

   _____

   _____

   _____

2. The "baptism in the Spirit" is a source of needless controversy in the church because two opposing sides use the
   phrase to define two different aspects of the baptism. What
   are they?

   a. _____

      _____

      _____

   b. _____

      _____

      _____

3. What are the steps to practically experiencing the "baptism
   in the Spirit" which is ours in Yeshua?

   a. _____

      _____

   b. _____

      _____

c. _____

_____

4. In discerning the leading of the Spirit we must always remember a crucial test to protect us in case we misinterpret the Spirit's leading. What is it?

_____

_____

5. The test of spirituality is the presence of: _____

_____

6. The fruit of the Spirit is: _____

_____

VERSES FOR MEMORIZATION

Romans 8:9,10,16
Ephesians 5:18
Romans 8:28
Galatians 5:16,22,23

SECTION C—THE WORD OF GOD

In this section, you will learn why we believe the Bible is the Word of God and how to practically profit from it. The Bible is the foundation of our spiritual knowledge, a living book quickened to our hearts by the Spirit.

Why do we believe the Bible is the Word of God? There are many reasons. The Bible is really a compilation of many writings from various prophets, apostles, and even kings. Yet it is unified in its moral and spiritual teaching, supernatural in its prediction, wonderful in the power of its promises, and majestic in its great description of the acts of God in the history of its peoples.

When we say the Bible is God's Word we mean God so oversaw and controlled the writing of Scripture that what the biblical writer taught was according to what God wanted to convey. At times God actually spoke to the writer and said, "Write these words." This was the case with the scroll Jeremiah produced for Jehoiakim under God's command (Jeremiah 36:1,3). At other times the writer produced material for instruction, worship, or correction (under the inspiration of the Spirit). The writer's style and personality was used by God to convey His message. Hence we read:

> "All Scripture is given God-breathed and is useful for teaching, rebuking, correcting and training in righteousness, so that the man of God may be thoroughly equipped for every good work." (II Timothy 3:16,17)

The word "inspiration" in Greek actually means "breathed out" by God. We want to list here several reasons why we believe the Bible is the Word of God.

(The student can more thoroughly study these reasons in more extensive writings if he wishes.)

1. *The unity of the Bible*—Although written by as many as 40 writers over a span of 2,000 years, the Bible gives evidence of amazing unity. It is fully consistent in its majestic doctrines of God and His nature, moral and social righteousness, and salvation by grace. Within it, many separate books claim to be God's Word.

2. *The fulfilled prophecy of the Bible evidences its super-natural character*—We include the prophecies of the Messiah's life, death, and resurrection in this discipleship course. There are also amazing predictions of the future of cities, sometimes in intricate detail. Scripture predicts the present regathering of Israel and its preservation (Isaiah 11:1,2; Ezekial 37), the ultimate end of Babylon as a city and kingdom (Jeremiah 50:51), and the intricate details of the future of Tyre (Ezekiel 26). These fulfillments took place over hundreds of years, and these are only a few examples of many such predictions and fulfillments.

3. *The archaeological accuracy of the Bible is another evidence of its trustworthy character*—Whenever archaeology provides information for reconstructing the history of the biblical period, it is always consistent with the biblical account. Nelson Glueck, the famous archaeologist, said there is not one archaeological finding which confutes a single biblical statement. When one considers the backward state of historical writing in the rest of the world, we are brought to the conclusion God was indeed in control of the writing of the Bible.

4. *Yeshua the Messiah, who rose from the dead, taught the full inspiration of the Tenach and provided for the New Testament by giving teaching authority to His apostles*—Yeshua said:

> "Do not think that I have come to abolish the Law or the Prophets (a common name for Scripture); . . . I tell you the truth, until heaven and earth disappear, not the smallest letter, not the least stroke of a pen, will by any means disappear from the Law until everything is accomplished." (Matthew 5:17,18)

In John 10:35, Yeshua said, "The Scripture cannot be broken." He constantly quoted Scripture with the preface "God said." We cannot accept Yeshua as our supreme teacher and reject His teaching on the Bible.

In John 14:25, He promised His disciples the anointing of the Spirit in a special way so they might accurately recount the teaching of Yeshua and receive further revelation.

5. *The Spirit of God witnesses to the heart of the believer*

that the Bible is the Word of God—When the believer reads the Bible he senses the very presence and power of God in it.

The books we accept as inspired are the books of the Tenach, known as the Old Testament in Christian circles. *These are books which Jewish tradition tells us come from the ancient prophets*, such as Moses, David, Jeremiah, Ezekiel, and Samuel. The New Testament books are those which come from the disciples of Yeshua, or those accepted into their circle of authority, such as Jude, James, and Paul. Luke wrote under the authority of Paul. *The witness of history in the writings of the Church Fathers (e.g., Papias, Eusebius) testifies to the apostolic origins of these books.*

Furthermore, *the early believers universally sensed the unique spiritual quality of the books we have in our New Testament.* Any believer can read a few of those books not accepted as authentic and compare them with the biblical books. The difference is vast and immediately apparent. The books we accept as inspired authority are called *canonical (having legal authority).* We have 66 books in our canon.

The Bible was given by the Spirit of God (I Peter 1:20,21) and is our final authority for teaching and morals. Because it is for the purpose of "training us in righteousness" (II Timothy 3:16), it is important every believer know how to read, study, and practically use the Bible. The beginning of growth in the Word is the incorporation into every believer's life of a daily quiet time with God.

The daily quiet time is a period of time set apart for prayer and reading the Word every day. With most people, no other time but morning is really workable. The morning quiet time takes place before we go to the work of the day. It prepares us mentally and spiritually for the whole day. We have never known any believer to become mature and spiritual without this daily period with God. The Word is the basic spiritual food for spiritual growth.

"Like newborn babies, crave pure spiritual milk (of the Word), so that by it you can grow up in your salvation." (I Peter 2:2). As you progress in the Lord, you will tailor your quiet time to your own personal needs and proclivities. Some people add a chapter from a good spiritual book, others vary their proportions of prayer and the Word. Our desire at this point is simply to give clear directions for establishing a quiet time.

First of all, find a quiet place to use regularly for your quiet time. Secondly, discipline yourself, at least on the weekdays, in beginning your quiet time at the same time every day. Plan your time in relationship to prayer and the Word. If your quiet time is one-half hour, perhaps plan on 15 minutes each, if an hour, perhaps 35 for reading the Word and 25 for prayer.

1. We recommend beginning with a brief period of praise and prayer. If there are any unconfessed known sins, they must be confessed and renounced before you can have fellowship with God. Come before God in the Name of Yeshua, on the basis of His blood atonement. Remember you never enter into God's presence on the basis of your own achievement, but neither are you precluded for lack of it.

Praise God! Thank Him for His faithfulness for His salvation in Yeshua, for His presence in the Spirit. Then ask the Holy Spirit to make the Word clear to you and to speak specifically to your heart.

2. The second step is reading the Word. It is very important you follow a specific plan of reading. There are plans available through many organizations. There is a Bible reading plan in the Messianic Jewish *Open Bible* put out by the Messianic Vision. You can create your own plan by deciding how many chapters you want to read each day and alternating between New Testament and Old Testament books. You should read the same book until you finish it. Your goal is not to read a large quantity of the Word, but to read an amount you can meditate upon.

Carefully read the passage. After you read, it is helpful to ask several questions. What did the passage say? Summarize it in your own mind. What promises, principles, or lessons can I receive from this passage? Sometimes this question is hard to answer for some passages. Pray and seek the answer. Many people find it valuable to record their findings in a personal journal.

Although important inspired material for study, genealogies, lists and obscure passages are not recommended for the new believer for quiet time. These passages can be worked with in another time of study. *We also strongly recommend under-lining passages which are important to you.* Some people use symbols or different colors to indicate prophecy, promises, and commands. Especially mark verses you want to memorize. If you do not have time, you can write the verses on cards at a later time.

3. Step number three is the prayer period. Ecclesiastes warns us not to come to God with many words (5:1-2). So sit quietly for a time to hear from God. Remember, prayer is not a monologue or a shopping list; it is a conversation. After entering into a time of praise, and perhaps praying in tongues if you use the gift, your first prayer concern is the passage you just read. The lessons from the Word should be prayed into your life. Visualize yourself living them out. You should also meditate on any promises in the passage and in Yeshua's Name claim them as your own if they apply to you. Allow the Holy Spirit to convict you of the truth and empower you to act it out.

Then spend more time in praise; praise is the power of prayer. It brings assurance for our petitions. Bring your requests before God. Begin with those who are close to you, your family and friends. Continue with prayer for your con-gregation and its leaders. Praying for the unsaved with whom you are in contact is crucial. It's helpful to make a prayer list.

Seek the Spirit's leading in what and whom you should pray for. Your prayers should be predominantly for the exten-sion of God's Kingdom, your love for God, and concern for others. God has promised to take care of you. You may pray about personal needs, but remember powerful prayer is not self-centered!

Be persistent in your requests until you either are con-vinced by the Spirit to no longer pray for a request or it is answered. God promises to answer prayer. His promises are remarkable!

Other aids in quiet time are written prayers and psalms which you can make your own by verbalizing them to God. This kind of prayer sets your mind into a positive focus. Great pray-ers teach us to pray. Some people call praying written prayers of promise, positive confession.

The quiet time is a faith builder. It starts your day off right and changes the whole nature of your daily life. Quiet time is *a necessity for spiritual growth.*

It is also valuable to incorporate periods of Bible study into your life. Bible study emphasizes learning. There are several different ways to study the Bible. A good way to start Bible study is to get a good study Bible. We recommend the *Open Bible* in the Messianic Jewish edition or Thompson's Chain Reference Bible. These study Bibles are unprejudiced in their viewpoint and provide valuable study aids such as indices, concordances (location of words used in the Bible), outlines, introductions, and cross references.

Remember this rule for Bible study: *the meaning of a passage is objectively determined by seeking to understand what the author intended to teach. This is determined by understanding his words in the context of the language meanings of the time in which it was written.* A good translation tries to convey the original meaning in English. But you need to understand that the original Hebrew and Greek convey the most accurate meaning. Also, remember the rule of context. Words are understood in the context of sentences, sentences in the context of paragraphs, and paragraphs in the context of the whole book. Here are several valuable Bible study methods:

1. *Book Study*—In book study one tries to learn the content of a book of the Bible. It is good to learn an outline of the book and to read the book several times. A good book or commentary written on the book can add to your insight of what is obscure to you.

2. *Subject Study*—In subject study a subject index is used to find and organize the teaching of several passages on a particular subject. By subject study we can understand what the Bible teaches on any topic of interest or concern.

3. *Word Study*—A concordance (a list of the use of words) is useful in finding all the passages where a particular word is used. In this way you can understand a biblical concept such as "flesh," "spirit," "salvation," "hate," or "sin." It is important however, to look up *words which are the same in the original language,* not just the same in English. A good concordance makes note of this.

Also remember, words have many definitions according to

the context in which they are used. Do not make the mistake of thinking the definition of a word in every passage is the same. This can lead to serious mistakes.

4. *Character Study*—This type of study traces the life of a prominent Bible character. In this way you can understand the person and the lessons to be learned from his or her life.

(The student should be aware of helpful tools for Bible study. Bible dictionaries, with articles on various subjects, concordances, commentaries, and topical books on biblical subjects are helpful. Pick books produced by believers gifted in the area of ministry related to their writings. We recommend as a start the one volume *New Bible Commentary* and the *New Bible Dictionary*. Bible handbooks such as Unger's, Halley's, and Eerdman's are also helpful.)

We want to encourage you in the Word. It gives life! The Psalmist said,

> "I have hidden Your word in my heart that I might not sin against You." (Psalm 119:11)
> "Oh how I love Your law! I meditate on it all day long." (119:97)
> "They are sweeter than honey, than honey from the comb. By them is Your servant warned; in keeping them there is great reward." (19:10,11)

Psalm 19 also tells us the Word makes the simple wise, revives the soul, and enlightens the eyes. Joshua said,

> "Do not let this Book of the Law depart from your mouth; meditate on it day and night, so that you may be careful to do everything written in it. Then you will be prosperous and successful." (Joshua 1:8)

STUDY QUESTIONS

List five reasons we believe the Bible is God's Word.

a. _____

b. _____

c. _____

d. _____

e. _____

2. Define the word "canonical." _____

_____

3. List several reasons we accept just the books we do as part of the Bible.

_____

_____

_____

4. List several reasons a quiet time is very important.

_____

_____

_____

5. Name and define briefly the four types of Bible study mentioned.

a. _____

_____

b. _____

_____

c. _____

_____

d. _____

_____

6. Summarize the procedure for having a quiet time.

_____

_____

_____

_____

VERSES FOR MEMORIZATION

Joshua 1:8
Psalm 119:11
II Timothy 3:16,17
I Peter 2:2

IV. HOLINESS AND POWERFUL PRAYER

SECTION A—THE MARKS OF HOLINESS

In the past chapters we defined holiness as *separation from the ways of the world system unto God and His ways*. The true disciple of Yeshua is called to a righteous life according to Scripture's standard. Scripture makes it clear that progress on the way to holy living is a prerequisite for powerful prayer. James said, "The prayer of a righteous man is powerful and effective." (James 5:16b).

Scripture also says, "You are to be holy, because I, the Lord, am holy . . . ." (Leviticus 20:26). What are the marks of holiness? They are not as the world so often thinks, dark clothing, glum faces, and external pretentious shouts of piety. A holy person is a person of deep joy.

We need to understand there has been a horrible decline of morality the past few decades. Through the influence of the media, this decline has been more rapid than any other decline in history. Hedonistic ways are encouraged on most television shows. Often believers are deceived into thinking they maintain adequate standards of conduct. However, when one looks at the standards of the past 300 years or even 3,000 years of biblical history, one recognizes how *the ways of the world have crept in among us, destroying our joy and power*. We have become more grossly evil. The believing community has kept itself separate from the world not by keeping only slightly better standards than the world. Believers have adopted hand-me-down standards of the world and therefore stay only slightly behind the trends. We could diagram it like this:

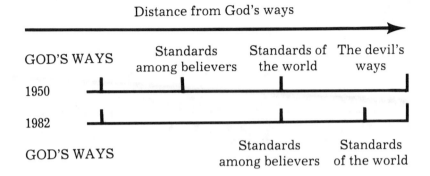

As the world gets worse, our standards as believers need to become higher, not proportionately lower. Our standard is the holy Word of God, not keeping only so far behind the world. Let us look at biblical marks of holiness.

1. *A holy person is one who has died to self.* Yeshua said,

> "If anyone would come after Me, he must deny himself and take up his cross daily and follow me. For whoever wants to save his life will lose it, but whoever loses his life for me will save it. What good is it for a man to gain the whole world, and yet lose or forfeit his very self?" (Luke 9:23-25)

In Scripture, to lose self does not mean to lose personal identity. It means to lose self-seeking motivations. When we identify with the death and resurrection of Yeshua, we replace selfish motives with motives of unselfish love and compassion. We love God with all our hearts and our neighbors as ourselves.

According to Luke, there must be a daily recommitment to this way of the cross. The way of love must not be identified with other forms of attachment called love. Infatuation may care for the other so it can possess the other for itself. Biblical love is care and compassion without possessiveness: it is not jealous, boastful, or proud (I Corinthians 13). Biblical love perseveres in difficulty, it is patient and kind. Yeshua in us produces this love.

(The student should take time now to read I Corinthians 13.)

2. *A holy person is a person of compassionate love (agape).* This second characteristic is simply implied from the first characteristic.

3. *A holy person reflects God's standards of righteousness in the Bible.* Because Messiah is in us, Paul said the way of faith fulfills the law (Romans 3:31). The believer does not sin so grace may abound, but he understands grace as the power of righteousness (e.g., he reflects honesty in business, love for the poor, and honoring the aged). We cannot outline all of God's standards but want to mention a specific area of concern in our day: *sexual morality.*

The Bible is absolutely clear that a sexual relationship is a beautiful gift of God reserved for *marriage.* Physical involvements which excite sexual feeling before the commitment of marriage are *called fornication* in the Bible.

God is a faithful God and *He created marriage to reflect His covenant faithfulness.* God hates adultery and divorce! The world says you need sexual experience to test compatibility. The Bible says love is the fruit of commitment. Friendship precedes love. Sexual involvement is just a diversion from building a real friendship.

There is no area in which society stands farther removed from traditional moral standards than in the area of sexual relationships. We are not referring to just narrow Puritan standards. For 3,000 years righteous people have had safeguards against pre-marital sexual involvement. Men and women were always chaperoned, never allowed in homes alone. Dates were always with another couple. Sufficient privacy was allowed so friendship could be formed, but not enough privacy for sexual intimacy. *This was universal for 3,000 years!* (during periods when Judeo-Christian morality prevailed).

Some believers have bought the myth that we need physical intimacy before marriage. This shows how the world has deceived us. The believer should take this into account in prayerfully forming clear moral standards.

Because sex is a holy gift, Scripture encourages us to be modest in our dress (I Peter 3:1-6). Modesty does not call attention to one's self in such a way as to excite sexual passion in another (e.g., tight clothing, the braless look), but calls attention to the face. The face should reflect the joy and love of God. This turns the mind to the spiritual and beautiful. Scripture also enjoins distinctive clothing for men and women; not necessarily slacks verses dresses, but distinct masculine and feminine styles.

Maintaining sexual purity requires discipline over our minds. We are to dwell on what is pure, lovely, noble, and right (Philippians 4:8ff), or we can fall into a lustful heart. Entertainment which calls attention to the sexual is of no purpose to the believer. This is difficult today because literature, television, and movies are so inundated with sex it seems as though it is of supreme value in our society! A discriminating believer carefully selects what he reads and sees, remembering the biblical injunction to flee youthful lusts.

A word should be said here about masturbation. Few people can masturbate without fantasizing. Both fantasy and masturbation are a habitual bondage trap and all bondage is to be avoided (I Corinthians 6:12, Romans 6:16). Some people consider masturbation as merely a physical release. But the problem which requires a physical release such as masturbation is lack of control over *one's thoughts*. Masturbation is totally self-centered and does not come under the category of denying self. If you have a problem with masturbation, do not compound it by going on a guilt trip. It is one sin among others, and with prayer, the Word, and disciplining your thoughts, you can overcome it; many people have.

We close this brief section on sexual morality be quoting I Corinthians 6:18-20:

> "Flee from sexual immorality. All of the sins a man commits are outside his body, but he who sins sexually sins against his own body. Do you not know that your body is a temple of the Holy Spirit, who is in you, whom you have received from God? You are not your own; you were bought with a price. Therefore honor God with your body."

4. *A holy person does not lust for material possessions.*
Scripture promises that God will abundantly provide whatever
we need for whatever He calls us to do. If His calling includes
material gifts of wealth, we praise Him and use our wealth for
His Kingdom. If not, we still praise Him. Some people give
foolish defenses of worldly materialism. Paul said,

> "I know what it is to be in need, and I know what
> it is to have plenty. I have learned the secret of being
> content in any and every situation, whether well fed
> or hungry, whether living in plenty or in want. I can
> do everything through Him who gives me strength."
> (Philippians 4:12,13) (c.f. esp. I Timothy 6:3-10)

God has promised to provide and we should be so caught up
in loving and serving, we are just not preoccupied with things!
We have known some believers to squander God's money with
uncontrollable urges for adult toys; avoid this.

5. *A holy person is called to holy or pure thinking.* God's
standard of holiness includes purity of thought. Scripture
teaches that out of the heart (the thought center), flow "evil
thoughts, murder, adultery, sexual immorality, theft, false testimony, slander. These are what make a man 'unclean' " (Matthew 15:19,20).

The Bible tells us to bring every thought into the captivity
of the Messiah (II Corinthians 10:5). Wrong ideas may come into
our minds at times, this is the one way the devil attacks us. But
we have the power to repel the devil's attack and control our
minds. The key way to do this is keeping an attitude of prayer
and thanksgiving at all times and in all circumstances before
God (I Thessalonians 5:18, Ephesians 5:20). When we are not
engaged in attending to work, we are not to let our minds drift
to evil thoughts of hate, bitterness, revenge, lust, or how someone has wronged us. We are to pray in love for our enemies and
make an effort to think godly thoughts in the power of the
Spirit. Paul wrote,

> "Finally, brothers, whatever is true, whatever is
> noble, whatever is right, whatever is pure, whatever

is lovely, whatever is admirable—if anything is excellent or praiseworthy—think about such things." (Philippians 4:8)

There is so much in God's creation and in His kingdom to preoccupy us with good. This kind of thinking leads to joy. Why give ourselves to thinking which is of no benefit? Even the temporary satisfaction of evil thoughts destroys our bodies, fills us with guilt, and ruins our joy and fellowship with God. *The first and central question for the depressed, anxious, angry, or lustful, is what do you give your mind to think? Victory in this area is victory everywhere!*

6. *The holy person is called to purity of speech.* The biblical standard for speech is summarized in Ephesians 4:29,30. Speech flows from thought.

> "Do not let any unwholesome talk come out of our mouths, but only what is helpful for building others up (edify) according to their needs, that it may benefit those who listen. And do not grieve the Holy Spirit of God, with whom you were sealed for the day of redemption."

Many carnal (worldly, unholy) believers engage in lewd jokes or off-color remarks. This indicates a mind which makes unwholesome connections. Cursing, lewd talk, gossip, slander, and negative tearing-down, are all examples of unholy talk. *God expects our speech to reflect reverence for Him, reverence for human beings created in His image, and reverence for His creation.*

Lewd talk and off-color jokes demean the beauty of God's creation of sexuality. They undercut the wonder and worship which is the proper response to this gift. Gossip and slander undercut respect for human beings created in God's image. The preoccupation of today's youth with "potty language"-cursing also undercuts the value of man. Cursing is slander against God and His creation.

The person who learns purity of speech has the ability to rejoice in the works of God. Those with critical, suspicious speech ruin relationships of love and trust. They divide people and cause discord. With their actions they cut down and destroy instead of building up in the Lord. This is why James compared the tongue to the rudder of a ship.

> "The tongue also is a fire, a world of evil among the parts of the body . . . he, however, who can control his tongue can bring his whole being under control." (James 3:6ff.)

The holy person is called to humility. Genuine holiness cannot be maintained apart from humility. *The proud person may externally follow some of the rules of holiness but will project a self-righteous, holier-than-thou attitude.* Humility is not self-deprecation. Self-deprecation is a manifestation of insecurity and self-rejection. Humility is an attitude of dependence and gratitude toward God. It includes an accurate self-appraisal which sees God's standard, seeks to grow, but recognizes that all accomplishment is by His grace.

The humble person accepts himself in the Messiah. He also has an attitude of listening and learning before others. The humble person rejects sin and grieves over it, but he projects love and acceptance toward the other person. We are all created by God, are of equal worth, and are all saved by His grace.

Often people feel convicted of sin before the words and life of a holy person. This was so in the life of Yeshua. People didn't feel that kind of arrogant superiority which dismisses others as less significant. *Holiness without humility is pretense.* Without holiness and humility you cannot help others conquer sin and grow into maturity.

8. *The holy person is a socially compassionate person.* Nothing is clearer from a study of the prophets than the fact that God seeks legal and economic justice for the poor, widowed, orphaned, and alienated. We do not endorse a particular philosophy. Honest believers differ as to which plans will work. But what they must not differ in is that Christians are called to be advocates of social justice and compassion. A holy person is also honest and compassionate in his own financial dealings.

Holiness is a prerequisite to powerful prayer. Thus our first prayer should be, "Make me a holy person in the Messiah." James says, "the effectual, fervent prayer of a righteous man availeth much." (James 1:16). Holiness is achieved by drawing on the power of the Spirit, because we are in the Messiah.

STUDY QUESTIONS

1. Holiness is _____

_____

_____

2. Sexual purity is commanded because God created marriage

to _____

_____

3. What is Scripture's promise in regard to material prosperity?

_____

_____

_____

4. God expects our speech to reflect reverence. What are we to

show reverence toward? _____

_____

_____

5. What are the results when a proud person follows some of the

rules of holiness? _____

_____

_____

_____

VERSES FOR MEMORIZATION
James 1:16
I Corinthians 6:19
Ephesians 4:29
Micah 6:8

SECTION B—PRAYER AND FAITH

The Scripture's promises on prayer and faith are wonderful. Every follower of Messiah is given the opportunity of walking by faith and prayer in a truly satisfying life.

Faith, a deep spiritual confidence or trust in God and His Word, is the prerequisite for answered prayer. Faith actually enables one to command the very elements of nature. Yeshua said,

> "I tell you the truth, if you have faith as small as a mustard seed, you can say to this mountain, 'Move from here to here' and it will move. Nothing will be impossible for you." (Matthew 17:20)

In another passage, Yeshua said faith enables us to cast the mountain into the sea (Matthew 21:21-22). Other Scriptural promises are just as exciting. Look at the following:

> "I tell you the truth, anyone who has faith in Me will do what I have been doing. He will do even greater things than these, because I am going to the Father. And I will do whatever you ask in My Name, so that the Son may bring glory to the Father. You may ask Me for anything in My Name, and I will do it." (John 14:12-14)

> "This is the assurance we have in approaching God: that if we ask anything according to His will, He hears us. And if we know that He hears us—whatever we ask—we know that we have what we asked of Him." (I John 5:14-15)

Faith is a necessity for any successful approach to God. Hebrews 11:6 says, "And without faith it is impossible to please God, because anyone who comes to Him must believe that He exists and that He rewards those who earnestly seek Him."

The nature of faith, as Scripture speaks of it, is not emotionally psyching ourselves up to believe whatever we want.

Faith is nurtured in the receptive heart by the Holy Spirit. Romans 10:17 says, "Faith comes from hearing the message, and the message is heard through the Word of Messiah."

The Holy Spirit takes *the Word and makes it alive* to the receptive heart. We then find a conviction in our heart so we are able to claim God's promises by faith as we pray.

We want to explain these promises more fully. They are not blank checks to ask for any outrageous thing we might desire. Rather there are several, often unrecognized, qualifications in these promises on prayer. They are to ask "according to God's will" or in the *Name* of Yeshua.

To the Eastern mind, a person's *name* represented the meaning and essence of the person. *To ask in Yeshua's Name is to ask on the basis of the authority of His Name since we are in Him. To use the name of an authority rightly, it must be used according to the character and expressed desire of the person whose name we use.*

God does not give us believing faith for any request which is contrary to His written Word. He will not answer prayers which are selfishly motivated (James 4:3). We come before God in the Name of Yeshua because only by His redemption and in His authority do we have the right to come.

The first step to successful prayer is listening to God's Spirit through the Word in terms of what we should pray. Psalm 37:4 says, "Delight yourself in the Lord and He will give you the desires of your heart." When we delight ourselves in the Lord, our desires change into a reflection of His desires.

In loving God, spending time in His Word, and listening to His Spirit, we find our heart's primary desire is to love and serve God better. We desire the extension of His kingdom, that people come to know and become like the Messiah. Thus our prayers will emphasize concern for the lost and for the growth of our brothers and sisters in the Messiah. As we reflect on what to pray during our quiet time, God's Spirit gives us a sense or burden of just the things we are to pray for. Not everyone can pray for everything; each person has his own prayer list.

Scripture enjoins us to pray for such things as our congregational leaders, governmental leaders, the prosperity of our congregations, and the peace of Jerusalem. Most requests of a specific nature, however, are laid on our hearts by the Spirit. Of all the unsaved people I know, for whom should I pray? Whom should I pray for in regards to growth? For which ministries should I pray? We all need to search our spirits in this matter. If God leads us to pray for a mountain to be cast into the sea, it will be done.

There are also many wonderful promises in Scripture for God's financial provision, for health, for the ability to accomplish tasks we are given by God (Philippians 4:13), and for the salvation of our families. These also are matters for which we should reflect on the Word and allow sufficient faith to grow in us so we can pray in faith.

Remember, faith is not psyching yourself up, but simply allowing the Holy Spirit to speak to you through the Word or by His "still, small voice," (I Kings 19:12,13) and implant faith (conviction) in your heart. Faith may or may not be accompanied by emotional feelings.

Some people make a distinction that helps us pray in faith. *The written Word, called in Greek, "logos," must become a Word spoken to our heart by the Spirit if it is to produce faith. All of the written Word is God's revelation, but faith requires the work of the Spirit. When the Spirit speaks we hear a "rhema," or a word activated by the Spirit.* The word "rhema" is the word used in Romans 10:17 where we understand that faith comes by hearing or receiving the Word (rhema). Receptive prayer and Scriptural meditation provide the setting in which we can receive "rhema."

Another ingredient essential to successful prayer is perseverance. *We are not to give up until we have the sense from God that we have "prayed through." This sense usually comes when God has granted the request. Sometimes God delays His answer.* This tests our faith and our character grows. Yeshua taught this in Luke 18:1-8. Here He taught the lesson of praying and not giving up. In illustration of this, He told about a widow who kept at her request for justice before a reluctant judge. The judge finally complied. So much more is God willing to answer prayer.

God has determined prayer as the means through which He will work in the world. This is not because He is reluctant to act. *It is because He has promoted us to be the channels of His work.* Prayer is spiritual warfare. Through it we develop greater faith, by it we benefit from intensive character development. As a race we fell in Adam, therefore the redemption of the world becomes our responsibility in Yeshua. In Him we have the power to bring God's healing to the world.

There are many great stories of people who learned the lessons of prayer and faith. Some heard from God, gave up their last penny in love, assured of God's provision; they discovered miraculous supply. George Mueller in 19th century England prayed for God's provision for his orphanage. God led him to establish the orphanage to reflect His power and love. Mueller never sought to raise funds, he prayed in all the needed goods. Often when there were bills or specific needs, God provided gifts to the *exact* figures of the needs.

Others have built congregations of thousands by prayer and faith with miracle after miracle attending the building of the congregation. Certainly God is ready to meet your needs; fulfill His promises in you, and mightily answer your prayers. Just grow in the Word and Spirit so you learn to hear Him.

One other ingredient is necessary for building faith. It is prayer and thanksgiving, which some people call "positive biblical confession." This must be clearly distinguished from humanistic positive thinking. We base our positive approach on the commands and promises of Scripture. The Bible teaches we must discipline our thoughts and words so we can maintain a stance of praise and thanksgiving. We read in Ephesians 5:18b-20,

> "Be filled with the Spirit. Speak to one another with psalms, hymns and spiritual songs. Sing and make music in your heart to the Lord, *always giving thanks to God the Father for everything in the Name of our Lord Yeshua the Messiah.*"

In I Thessalonians 5:16-18, Paul wrote, "Be joyful always; pray continually; give thanks in all circumstances, for this is God's will for you in Messiah Yeshua."

This is a stumbling block to many people. The flesh tempts

us to respond to difficult circumstances, setbacks and even tragedies, not with words of praise, but with anger, doubt, and accusation against God and others. The attitude of praise and thanks is not "whistling in the dark." *It is rather the ability to find good in most circumstances because we know the Lord of Love and His promises.* This is the focus of our praise.

Even if we find nothing good in certain circumstances, we can praise God for Himself. If we are not in unrepented sin, we know we walk in His care. "And we know that in all things God works for the good of those who love Him, who have been called according to His purpose." Even the attacks of Satan are not beyond God's controlling power.

When Corrie Ten Boom found herself in a lice-infested Nazi concentration camp barracks, she praised God for the Bible in her possession and taught the women the Word. Trials are opportunities to show forth God's glory, to see Him work. "No temptation has seized you except what is common to man . . . God will also provide a way. . . ." (I Corinthians 10:13). The believer can praise God in all circumstances; financial reversals, betrayals, and even death, because he knows and believes God's Word. The promises of the Word are so great!

> "I can do everything through Messiah who gives me strength." (Philippians 4:13)

> "And my God will meet all your need according to His glorious riches in Messiah Yeshua." (Philippians 4:19)

> "All the promises of God are Yea and Amen in Yeshua." (II Corinthians 1:20)

This does not mean the believer walks around with a pasted-on smile without empathy for others. We are counseled to "weep with those who weep." But we are to praise God in the tears and even in sorrow because there is an inner confidence and peace when we walk in faith. The believer is called to a *positive, optimistic stance toward life.* God made us, we are of worth in Him. We are children of the King, joint heirs with

Messiah, destined to reign with Him. We are new creatures in the Messiah (II Corinthians 5:17). We have exactly those gifts and talents He desires us to have.

Many believers are kept from victorious living by negative thoughts about life, themselves, and others. Praise and thanks, positive confession with our lips about who we are in the Messiah, positive confession about His promises, is God's remedy for inferiority feelings, insecurity, depression, and anxiety. Positively confessing the Word is simply repeating the Word with our mouths and dwelling on it. Johanna Chernoff, wife of the spiritual leader of Beth Yeshua congregations in Philadelphia, counsels a morning regimen to set the pace of the day. This starts us off in joyous, exciting living. Upon arising, say, "This is the day the Lord has made, let us rejoice and be glad in it. Today will be a wonderful day for the Lord, I can do all things through Him. I am His beloved, a new creature in the Messiah, a joint heir."

Furthermore there are Scriptural promises we can repeat and use for every situation. There are scriptural teachings to draw upon and quote to defeat Satan in every temptation. The victory is ours in Yeshua!

Praise creates and bolsters faith. Praise is powerful. When we praise God in detail for who He is and what He has done, when we praise Him constantly, we defeat Satan. Our spirits are revived and we can most readily believe the promises of the Word.

Scripture teaches God inhabits the praises of His people (Psalm 22:3). Praise brings God's presence in a powerful way. Before His presence darkness must flee, for He is light. Let's walk in victory. Let's praise him and confess the Word concerning our worth in Him and His ability in us. Then He will lay upon our hearts requests for intercessory prayer and our prayers will be answered.

STUDY QUESTIONS

1. What is biblical faith? _____

   _____

   _____

   _____

2. What does it mean to ask "in the Name of Yeshua?" _____

   _____

   _____

3. Distinguish between the two terms for Word, "logos" and

   "rhema." _____

   _____

   _____

   _____

4. Why can we praise God in and for all things? _____

   _____

   _____

   _____

   _____

5. What does it mean to persevere in prayer? _____

_____

_____

_____

_____

VERSES FOR MEMORIZATION
Philippians 4:13,14
John 14:12-14
I John 5:13-15
Ephesians 5:18-20

SECTION C—APPLYING FAITH AND PRAYER

In the last section, we emphasized the importance of building faith by praise and thinksgiving. This is amazingly in accord with ancient Jewish tradition. This tradition developed words of praise and thanksgiving for every situation, from seeing the beauties of creation to events of sorrow and death. This brings us to the topic of the value of written prayer. *The purpose of written prayer is to deepen the content of praise and worship. It is to be an inspiration for our own spontaneous praise and worship.*

Many of us find our prayers become rote, that little content comes into our minds for praise. Our minds wander. To avoid this, we suggest the incorporation of written prayer material into your prayer life. But remember, the purpose of written prayer is thwarted if it is used as a rote exercise instead of your own genuine expression. We are to leap from the written prayer to our own expression of praise. Slowly lift the praises up to God and picture what you are praising for. Continue until you sense a spontaneous flow from the Spirit arising in your heart.

There are many good sources of written prayer. Here are a few examples:

1. The Psalms—These are certainly an excellent source for praise and worship. They contain faith-building promises as well as a variety of topics for praise and thanksgiving.
2. The Siddur—This Jewish prayer book is 80 percent Scripture, or Scripture passages woven together. It provides praise and thanksgiving material as well as positive confession in terms of God's promises.
3. Prayers developed by other Spirit-filled believers— These direct us to praise and positive confession of God's Word for all circumstances. Examples of these are:
   a. Peter Lord's *2959 Prayer Devotions Method.* This is highly recommended.
   b. The prayers of warfare and positive confession in Mark Bubeck's, *The Adversary.* (Moody)

Incorporating periods in our lives of increasing our receptivity to hearing the Spirit is essential for a successful life of prayer. It is in the atmosphere of praise that we receive God's Word for any need or situation. To receive blessings from God, it goes without saying we must be living in accordance with His will by the power of His Spirit. Right motives must permeate our prayers. We should be motivated by the love of God, the desire for His glory, and a love and compassion for others. Let's apply this to a few key areas of human need.

Many desire very deeply that their parents, children and friends come to a knowledge of the Messiah. To pray in faith for unsaved loved ones, it is useful to follow the following guidelines:

First of all, pray that you are consistent in your love and testimony to the truth. Your first prayer for their salvation might be that God would change you more. Do you need to ask their forgiveness? Have you acted in love toward them? We should not be motivated only by a fleshly attachment to them, but rather by agape (selfless love) and godly compassion. How can we tell the difference? Many people, especially parents, often ask God's mercy on their children as if they really have valid excuses for their sin, rebellion and unconcern for the things of God. The parent's concern is not primarily for God's glory, but in defense of the sinner before God. Every sinner, no matter what the circumstances of his life, is responsible before God. Compare these two prayers:

1. "Oh, God, have mercy on my lost son. You know what a hard life he's had. It seems as if he can't help himself. You know as a child others mistreated him, so do not judge his faults, but consider his weakness and save him, in Yeshua's Name."

2. "Oh, God, I come to you seeking your salvation and mercy for my son in the Name of Yeshua. I confess he is in sin and rebellion against You, without excuse. Forgive my sins in the degree to which they thwarted his coming to repentance. I am grieved that his life is a shame to Your Name. Save him for Your glory. God of Love, have compassion and turn him to repentance. I

grieve for him, in Yeshua's Name."

Notice how the first prayer reflects wrong motives. In contrast, the second prayer reflects honesty, concern for God, and agape love.

Secondly it is helpful in praying for the lost to meditate on them and their terrible blindness and need. Visualize them healed according to what they *can be* in Yeshua. Seek a sense of the Spirit, in praise, and a burden of compassion from God. Persevering prayer will be answered. If you are God-inspired in your prayers you are assured of their success. God does not violate the freedom of the unbeliever, but when persistent believing prayer is offered, it is most likely the person will be saved. This is because our prayers bind the power of Satan who binds the unbeliever. It brings the convicting power of the Holy Spirit to bear fully on him. We see few people coming to the Lord because we pray for few people with real faith.

Physical healing is another area of concern for answered prayer. The covenant promises concerning physical well being in Scripture are amazing. These promises are rooted in Torah. It should be noted that Scripture teaches that all of the promises of God in the Messiah (from the Torah and the prophets) are "Yes in Him" (II Corinthians 1:20). The promises to those who abide in covenant obedience, abiding in the vine (Yeshua), are as follows:

> "If you will diligently hearken to the voice of the Lord your God, and do that which is right in his eyes, and give heed to his commandments and keep all his statutes, I will put none of these diseases upon you which I put on the Egyptians; for I am the LORD, your healer." (Exodus 15:26).

> "You shall serve the Lord your God, and I will bless your bread and your water; and I will take sickness away from you. None shall cast her young or be barren in your land; I will fulfill the number of your days." (Exodus 23:25,26).

The N.I.V. translates this as I will give you "the full span of your life." Hence, the atonement which procures the new covenant is spoken of as providing physical and spiritual healing.

> "He himself bore our sins in his own body on the tree that we being dead to sins might live unto righteousness by his wounds I have been healed" (I Peter 2:24).

Peter here quotes Isaiah 53 as applying to bodily healing while Matthew 8 applies the Isaiah passage to Yeshua's healing ministry.

Furthermore, James 5:14 speaks of the elders anointing with oil (a symbol of the work of the Holy Spirit) and "the prayer of faith will save the sick man and the Lord will raise him up; and if he has committed sins, he will be forgiven."

These passages then show that it is God's ultimate ideal and provision for believers to walk in divine health. However, it is well to note specifics in working this out in practical life.

God may permit sickness as a trial or affliction to draw us to Himself and His power to overcome it or to indicate sin. Hence, our first response to physical affliction should not necessarily be to immediately claim healing or to fear. Rather, we should seek God in prayer and in the Word to see if there is anything He is trying to say to us? Is there sin in some area of our lives? Are we outside of His will? Did God desire to redirect us but we were not listening?

Remember, the promise of healing accompanies abiding in the vine and walking in faith-obedience.

After searching these things out, possibly with others, we should search the Scriptures for its promises on healing. As we meditate on the written word it becomes in the Spirit's power God's word spoken to us or *Rhema*. As we confess out loud these healing promises and act upon them we are healed. The council of mature believers can be greatly helpful. They can stand with you in prayer. Scripture also calls upon us to call the elders to anoint the sick with oil (the symbol of the Spirit) and to pray for healing in accordance with James 5:14.

In general, Scripture makes it clear that it is God's will for us to be in good health. "By his stripes we have been healed" (Isaiah 53). However, we must never carelessly condemn another who is sick. Until God gives revelation, the complexities of a situation may be beyond our comprehension.

Visualizing is a real key to faith-prayer. Prayerful visualization and confession of the Word builds faith.

When we look at sickness in greater detail, we see a variety of reasons for it.

1. Sickness may be the result of sin—Bitterness, anxiety, unforgiveness—all these have detrimental effects on us physically. Not flowing in the Spirit with a local body of believers removes us from the protection and blessing which comes as a result of fellowship. The process of healing is both individual and communal.

2. Sickness may be due to abuse of the body—God will graciously heal when we repent and change our ways. However, gluttony, rich foods, smoking, and other poor habits take their toll. Our bodies are dwelling places of the Spirit to be taken care of (I Corinthians 6:19).

3. Sickness may be a trial to enable us to increase our faith—We are to grow in character by it and defeat the devil (I Corinthians 12:7-10).

In this life we grow to be like the Messiah. There is no perfect person in this life except in terms of his position in Messiah. There is therefore no perfection of healing. Unless the Messiah returns soon we will all die physically at least from aging. But although there is no perfect healing, there is substantial healing. As we walk in the Spirit and in love, we can expect to live a healthy and long life.

Another major area of concern in prayer is stewardship of finances. There are many great promises in the Scriptures in regard to material blessing. If we are following the Lord, we can in prayer claim these promises for financial success. However, to do so rightly, it is important we understand the full scope of the Bible's teaching on this.

Today there is some foolish teaching in regard to finances. Some people have been told if they tithe, they can confess in faith, all kinds of wealth, mansions, cars, expensive vacations, and large investment holdings. The reasoning behind this goes:

God has said if you give generously and are not lazy in your financial endeavors, He will give you abundant success (Joshua 1:8, Luke 6:3). Abundant success is then defined in terms of modern American prosperity. This teaching is perilously shallow and in danger of plunging us into a lust for material possessions when we are to *die to self* and live in love.

Scripture's teaching on material wealth is far different from this reasoning. It first of all warns that material wealth is a snare which causes many to fall. People who teach this "abundant financial success" thinking never quote Scriptures such as I Timothy 6:6-10:

> "But godliness with contentment is great gain. For we brought nothing into the world, and we can take nothing out of it. But if we have food and clothing, we will be content with that. People who want to get rich fall into temptation and a trap and into many foolish and harmful desires that plunge men into ruin and destruction. For the love of money is the root of all kinds of evil. Some people, eager for money, have wandered from the faith and pierced themselves with many griefs."

Matthew 6:19-21 says:

> "Do not store up for yourselves treasures on earth, where moth and rust destroy, and where thieves break in and steal. But store up for yourselves treasures in heaven, where moth and rust do not destroy, and where thieves do not break in and steal. For where your treasure is, there your heart will be also."

If we had only these teachings, we could go to the opposite extreme of believing it is wrong to be wealthy. But let's try to more adequately summarize biblical teaching and its relationship to faith and prayer.

1. *The Bible teaches wealth and material need is simply not to be our main concern.* Our heart's concern should be

loving God and others that we might extend His Kingdom.

(The student should here read Matthew 6:24-34. This passage teaches we are to trust our Heavenly Father to provide for us.)

The drift of Scripture's teaching is God will abundantly provide for whatever we need for whatever He calls us to do. And God has different callings. Our assurance, however, is that if we trust God and live for Him, He will provide.

2. *The Bible teaches all wealth is God's* (Deuteronomy 8:17,18). We are merely entrusted with wealth as stewards. We are to use it to provide for our families. If we do not, we are worse than infidels (I Timothy 5:8). However, we must recognize that beyond this our wealth should be used for the glory of God's Kingdom.

God may convince us He is giving us material gifts for our use, but this is not to be our *concern or preoccupation.* In Scripture, we are told to give generously a significant portion of our income. In the Tenach, this was in terms of the tithe or ten percent of one's income or production. In the New Covenant of grace, we are expected to give generously even beyond ten percent. We cannot outgive God.

> "Give, and it will be given to you. A good measure, pressed down, shaken together and running over, will be poured into your lap. For with the measure you use, it will be measured to you." (Luke 6:38)

In ancient Israel, the tithe supported the Temple ministries and the priests who taught the Word throughout Israel. We believe the tithe should go to one's local congregation and giving beyond ten percent should be given as the Spirit leads, whether to the local congregation or beyond.

As one minister put it, "You should primarily support your local body where you are fed and cared for. To not do so is like going to McDonald's and after eating, walking across the street and paying the bill at Burger King!"

3. *The Bible teaches we are to be financially responsible.* We are not to be a burden on the community. We are to work so we can give generously. Scripture teaches the community is

not to provide for anyone whose destitution is due to laziness. We are even told to avoid such a person (II Thessalonians 3:6-15).

4. *In faith and prayers, we can positively confess God will provide all of our financial needs if we are living in accordance with God's will as taught in the above sections.* We are amazed at how miraculously God provides for those who tithe generously and live by faith. We have seen unexpected funds provided for the exact amounts of outstanding bills, supernatural gifts of clothing which perfectly fit the need, and much, much more. God is faithful to provide.

Abundant provision is according to calling. Some believers are called to live modestly. Sharing communities have been formed in some cities to demonstrate how a community in God's love can share and have abundant life even though their personal wealth in net terms is small. To see the joy and richness in such communities is an eye-opener and faith stimulator.

Other people are called to a moderate lifestyle. They live in a suburban house, drive an adequate car, and give generously.

Some people have been called to handle great wealth for God's Kingdom. Their personal income is great, but it is used for the Lord. I know of people who are not extravagant with themselves contrary to God's will, just as there are some people who sin with their wealth.

We must recognize the amount of wealth an individual handles is a call of God. This call takes into consideration the person's knowledge and ability in financial matters as well as his ability to resist the temptations of wealth. He needs to be a person of great faith. Other gifts and callings are just as crucial. Most spiritual leaders, for example, are not wealthy, but find abundance because God greatly provides. It is important to allow for freedom and variation in regard to wealth.

Wealth should never be sought for itself, flaunted, or misused. Profligacy and extravagance are sin, because we are to be wise stewards of the resources of the earth and of all we are entrusted with. But we are not to judge others, because God does give gifts and a clear conscience to buy for one's self. This is a matter of the Spirit's leading.

We are stewards of our money; it is not our own. *All we are and have is His.* Beware of people who try to convince everyone that all are called to make large sums of money. God calls many people to spend their time doing other things besides making large sums of money.

We especially want to say a word to people who are having financial difficulties. If this is a persistent problem, you should seek the counsel of your leaders. Usually this problem comes from several sources:

1. *Lack of faith*—This may be manifest in not tithing. One person asked, "Should I tithe even if I am in debt?" The reply is, "Yes, if you want to get out of debt." Lack of faith in God's provision is seen in these manifestations:
   a. not tithing—God will not give to us if we do not give.
   b. a grasping attitude toward money fearfully holding onto what we have. This attitude eventually leads to difficulty.
2. *Uncontrollable urges to spend*—The person with this problem often finds a need to have new gadgets, clothes, tools, and toys to satisfy him. In this case, material things are providing satisfaction instead of spiritual things. Insecurity may be at the root of this problem.
3. *A poor self-concept*—This person does not believe in himself or God's ability and gifts in Him. Hence he expects only meager jobs and meager provision for life.
4. *Laziness*—The lazy person does not have the motivation to "get ahead" and to handle finances capably.

The solution to all these problems comes in confessing our worth in the Messiah as joint heirs, children of the King, sons of God. We must allow the Holy Spirit to implant faith in our hearts to believe the promises of the Word. We confess these promises and then act in faith, responsibly, and generously. The average American lives in great material abundance. God will meet every need, but not greed. Count on Him and see Him work by faith and prayer.

Another area of stewardship is time. Many people are given various amounts of money, but we are all given 24 hours a day. People often say they do not have enough time. This is foolish.

Of course they have enough time, everyone has the same amount. Stewardship of time is a matter of two things: discipline and hearing from the Spirit how to parcel out our time.

We all must give adequately to personal time alone with God, serving the body, quality family time, friendship and rest. Rest includes restorative activities.

Our problem is really not lack of time but the inability to hear the Spirit because we do not *prayerfully* plan our involvements. Each person must consider his individual gifts and talents and decide how much time he will spend with his family and when; what evenings he will give to the work of the body of believers—which committees or activities he will join beyond major services; when and how he will meet unbelievers and share the good news with them; when he will study and when will be given to entertainment.

Scheduling is crucial to balanced living. A schedule should be regularly re-evaluated in prayer. It also should be flexible enough for special things that come up which the Spirit convicts us to be part of. All of us must balance all of the responsibilities we are called to. A biblical life does not allow one to forsake the home for busy involvements outside the home. But neither does it allow us to become homebodies.

In closing this section on prayer and faith, we want to summarize some hindrances to answered prayer. If your prayers go seemingly unanswered, perhaps this list will help you.

1. Perhaps your request is from the *wrong motive*, as James says, you ask amiss seeking gain for yourself (James 4:3).
2. Perhaps you have not been led by the Spirit in your requests (I John 5:14ff). You must *pray in God's will.*
3. *Unconfessed sin* or continued patterns of serious sin hinder our prayers. James says the prayers of the righteous avail (James 5:16, Ps. 68). Bitterness and unforgiveness are key sins which hinder answered prayer.
4. Perhaps *God has said no* and is trying to explain His reason but you are not listening (see Paul's experience in II Corinthians 12:7-10).
5. Perhaps you are to *continue in prayer* for a longer period

to build faith and character. You may be giving up too quickly (Luke 18:1-8).

6. Perhaps you are not *asking with faith* and need to allow the Word and Spirit to create greater faith in you. In this case you should spend time in the Word and in prayer until you gain new conviction (Matthew 17:20).

7. Perhaps you are out of God's will. Are you flowing with the Spirit in your local congregation? *Are you in God's will* in your profession, where you are living, or who you are spending time with? When a person resists God's will, his prayers are hindered.

8. Are you giving due regard and care to your husband or wife (I Peter 3) or to the saints (I Cor. 11)?

The life of faith and prayer is the way to become like Yeshua. By this, we may share His joy and produce much fruit for His Kingdom.

STUDY QUESTIONS

1. What is the purpose and value of written prayers?

_____

_____

_____

2. How should the believer first respond to sickness? _____

_____

_____

3. Name four reasons for sickness.

a. _____

b. _____

c. _____

d. _____

4. Name four reasons for financial difficulties.

a. _____

b. _____

c. _____

d. _____

5. In the prayers for family salvation, we gave examples of two different prayers. One was unlikely to be answered. Why?

_____

_____

_____

VERSES FOR MEMORIZATION
Matthew 6:19
Luke 6:38

"LORD, TEACH US TO PRAY." (Luke 11:1)
Posture in Prayer-
Bowing: Genesis 24:26, Exodus 4:31, Isaiah 45:23
Kneeling: Isaiah 45:23, Daniel 6:10
On face: Numbers 20:6, Matthew 26:39
Standing: I Kings 8:22, Mark 11:25, Luke 18:11
Hands Lifted (I Tim 2).
Modes of Worship-
Dance: II Samuel 6:14, Psalm 149:3, Psalm 150:4
Clap: Psalm 47:1
Shout: Isaiah 12:6, Psalm 47:1, Zephaniah 3:14
Cry: Psalm 30:2, Jonah 3:8
Sing: Psalm 13:6, Psalm 30:4, Isaiah 12:5, Hebrews 2:12
Praise: Psalm 69:34, Psalm 147:1, Hebrews 13:15

Joyful noise: Psalm 66:1, Psalm 81:1, Psalm 95:1,2, Psalm 98:4
Tongues and understanding: I Corinthians 14:13-15
(Researched by M. Rudolph)

THE CALL TO COMMUNITY

V. THE CALL TO COMMUNITY—BODY LIFE

In this chapter, as well as in chapter six, we discuss the biblical and practical aspects of life in the body of believers. The congregation of Yeshua is central to God's purpose. Flowing with God's purpose requires that we be clear concerning congregational life.

SECTION A—THE CONGREGATION AS THE MANIFESTATION OF GOD'S SPIRIT

Scripture makes it abundantly clear that God desires to manifest His life and reality thorugh a society, or a community. God's choice of Abraham to be the father of a *great nation*, first established this truth. Israel as a nation would be the living demonstration of God's power. Her triumph over all obstacles would demonstrate that the God of Abraham is the Lord of all. Furthermore, life within the nation would reflect the character of God.

Love and justice are demonstrated in relationships among people. Israel, by its just laws, compassionate economic life, and unique religious system, would be a living social demonstration of the truth. The nations would marvel at a nation that had a God so great and laws so just.

A nation in the midst of the nations, a witness people, this was always God's intention for Israel. However, Israel did not fulfill this role during many periods of her history. But her failures would be replaced with success under the New Covenant. Under the New Covenant God would provide direction for living as well as the power of the Spirit for every person.

The Holy Spirit is the means of accomplishing God's will under the New Covenant. The law of God is written on our hearts and the Holy Spirit dwells in believers. (See Jeremiah 31:31ff and Ezekiel 36 for the promise of the New Covenant.)

God is a social being. It is therefore no wonder that the demonstration of redeemed life is social, the community of believers. Central to the New Covenant is a new institution to be planted in all nations. It was originally called the Kehillah of Yeshua or congregation of Yeshua. Yeshua chose 12 disciples to be the foundational teachers or original core of this new body.

Shortly before He died and rose again, Yeshua asked, "Whom do men say that I am?" Many answers were given, including John the Baptist, Elijah, Jeremiah, and one of the prophets. However, Simon Peter (Shimon Kepha) replied, "You are the Messiah, the Son of the living God." Yeshua assured Peter this was known to him only because of the revelation of God's Spirit in his heart. He went on to explain that He was the rock and the confession that He is Lord and Messiah would be the foundation of His new worldwide kingdom.

> "On this rock I will build my congregation," Yeshua said, "and the gates of Hades will not overcome it. I will give you the keys of the kingdom of heaven; whatever you bind on earth will be bound in heaven, and whatever you loose on earth shall be loosed in heaven." (Matthew 16:18,19)

To the congregation of Yeshua alone is given the power to defeat the forces of the devil, to bind them and loose men and women from their hold. Forgiveness and new life come through the preaching and teaching of the congregation. The body of believers is the manifestation of God's rule and His kingdom for this age.

Matthew 16:18,19 also records Yeshua's institution of the body of believers. It is helpful to trace the ensuing events which launched this new institution in power. First of all, there is the great prayer of Yeshua in John 17. In this prayer, Yeshua prayed for a oneness of agape (love) to be present among His disciples and all who believe in Him through their testimony. His words bear repeating:

> "That all of them may be one, Father, just as You are in me and I am in You. May they also be in us so that the world may believe that You have sent me." (John 17:21)

Yeshua is clear that the success of the Good News in which He is acknowledged as Messiah is dependent upon the oneness of His people. The oneness applies on every level, to families, to local congregations, and to the universal body of believers. The prayer of Yeshua was amazingly fulfilled in the first community of Jewish believers in Jerusalem. We read how the first company of 120 was in one accord and devoted themselves to prayer (Acts 1:14). On the day of Shavuoth (Pentecost) the Holy Spirit came upon them with power. We read,

> "Suddenly a sound like the blowing of a violent wind came from heaven and filled the whole house where they were sitting. They saw what seemed to be tongues of fire that separated and came to rest on each one of them. All of them were filled with the Holy Spirit and began to speak in other languages as the Spirit enabled." (Acts 2:2-4)

The first believers in Yeshua were baptized in the Holy Spirit and spoke the message of the gospel in languages they had never learned. They communicated to Jewish people from many lands and languages. After Peter gave the call for repentance and faith, 3,000 people responded and were baptized. We read of these that,

> "They *devoted* themselves to the *apostles' teaching* and to the *fellowship*, to the *breaking of bread and to prayer* . . . all the believers were together and had everything in common. Selling their possessions and goods, they gave to anyone as he had need. Every day they continued to meet together in the temple courts.

They broke bread in their homes and ate together ·
with glad and sincere hearts, praising God and enjoy-
ing the favor of all the people. *And the Lord added* to
their number daily those who were being saved."
(Acts 2:42-47)

Out of this community came a movement which turned the
world upside down. By the time we come to Acts 21, despite
persecution and scattering, this community had grown to tens
of thousands (myriads). *Their secret was the unity of the Spirit
and the bonds of love that flow from Him*. In Acts 2 it is also said
they gave themselves to the sound teaching of the apostles. This
is done today through teachers placed in every congregation.

They were also given to prayer and fellowship. Fellowship
implies the very deepest sharing of spiritual life together. As we
progress in our study of the New Covenant Scriptures we find
wonderful teaching on the body of believers.

First of all, we note that most of the epistles or letters of the
New Covenant Scriptures were written to various localized
communities of faith. Although every believer is part of the
invisible universal congregation of Yeshua, it is not possible to
attend the services of the universal body or go to hear the
spiritual leaders of the universal congregation. It is crucial that
every believer recognizes the only *manifestation* of the universal body is in *local expressions* of the body. The local body is
where the universal body is visible.

God's plan is that there be local expressions of His body
everywhere. The largest proportion of New Testament teaching on the body refers to the local congregation. Every believer
is called to be part of a local expression of the body. This will
become especially clear as we look at several passages of
Scripture.

Allow us to note at this point an attitude which is destructive to God's plan of manifesting Himself in congregations. This
is the attitude of the freelance uncommitted believer. He or she
moves from congregation to congregation with little desire to
build anywhere in specific. Although it is good to be acquainted
with other communities, the congregational "gypsy" misses the
benefits and disciplines God ordained to flow through the body.

God desires to build us into a people who know one another, and who serve together. Only in the stable interaction of a local community can we really become what God desires.

God speaks to each community in terms of where the general membership is along the path of growth. The teaching needed at "A" congregation may not be what is immediately needed at "B" congregation. However, God may deal later with this teaching at "B". The gypsy believer becomes confused after going from place to place, often becomes critical of many local bodies, and judges one for not doing as the other. But God has His timing. Love begins with those we walk with daily and weekly. How sad that some profess a love for the universal body when they are not able to love any local people of God. This attitude which produces no real solid commitment to a local body is destructive.

Let's now look at some of Scripture's foundational teaching on the local body. First of all, the gathered congregation at worship and prayer is *the* place of the fuller manifestation of God's Spirit. In I Corinthians 3:16,17, we read,

> "Don't you know that you yourselves are God's temple and that God's Spirit lives in you? If anyone destroys God's temple, God will destroy him; for God's temple is sacred, and you are that temple."

The context of this passage makes it clear Paul is talking about the local body. Previously, he described how he had laid the teaching foundation in this body as an Apostle. All were to be careful how they built upon the foundation or God's judgment would burn it up (I Corinthians 3:10-15).

The universal body can never be destroyed. This is clear in Yeshua's promise that the gates of hell would not prevail against it (Matthew 16). However, local expressions of the body can be destroyed. The destruction of a local body is a capital offense *because the gathered community is the place of the holiest manifestation of the Spirit* on earth.

In ancient Israel, the most holy room in the Temple was the center of God's presence. Now it is in the body. It is true that the Holy Spirit is present everywhere, but He is more distinctly present in manifestation in the gathered community.

In Psalm 84, the Psalmist said. "Blessed are those who dwell in Your House; they are ever praising You. Blessed are those whose strength is in You," and "I would rather be a doorkeeper in the house of my God than dwell in the tents of the wicked." The Psalmist was expressing his delight at the prospect of being in God's presence. It should be the heart desire of all of us.

By faith, we should expect to be in God's presence whenever we gather as a community for worship, fellowship, and the teaching of the Word. It is in flowing with the presence and manifestation of the Spirit in the body that we are renewed and anointed for our particular tasks in the Lord.

Secondly, Scripture makes it clear God wants us to build our lives in relationship to one another under established elder authority. A fuller outline of authority is presented in chapter six. Paul appointed elders to oversee the congregations he established and commanded Timothy to do the same. All were to submit their lives for correction, counsel and instruction within a biblically balanced context (Hebrews 13:7,17). Galatians 6:1,2 teaches that all members of the body are to correct and help one another in love and gentleness. Hence we are built into an extended family of Yeshua under His headship. Note Peter's analogy with the Temple in I Peter 2:5.

> "You also, like living stones, are being built into a spiritual house to be a holy priesthood, offering spiritual sacrifices acceptable to God through Yeshua the Messiah."

Our sacrifices are the praise and service we bring to the Lord. Every believer is called to responsible service to the local body. According to talent and supernatural gift, everyone should have a regular task. This can be in music, building repair, visitation, counseling, committee work, and other such tasks.

However, the purpose of all the areas of involvement is to accomplish two goals of the body. *The first goal is that men and women might come to know God and His Messiah.* This is outreach; to do outreach requires equipping the saints (Ephesians 4:11ff). The second goal is *that men and women would become in character and love like the Messiah.* These two goals should be the very heart motive of every believer, because in sharing these goals, they share the very values of God. To know God more deeply is to become like Him. This is the walk of faith.

So central is the "body" in New Testament teaching that it cannot be overemphasized. Salvation is even seen in terms of being planted in the body, or "baptized into one body" (I Corinthians 12:13). To be a believer apart from the body is just not an option in the New Testament. All are called to regular worship, service, and generous support. Thus we read in Hebrews 10:24,25:

> "And let us consider how we may spur one another on toward love and good deeds. Let us not give up meeting together, as some are in the habit of doing, but let us encourage one another—and all the more as you see the Day approaching."

The work of the body takes place through the gifts and ministries of God's Spirit. The way to serve in the Spirit is to exercise the gifts God has given. This is the topic of our next section.

We close with a reminder that the primary witness to the truth of the gospel, according to the prayer of Yeshua in John 17, is a committed community of faith which loves and serves together in His power. This community should be everyone's central concern. We cannot expect God's blessing if we knowingly rebel against His will in this regard. The blessings of God are for those who share in His values and purposes.

STUDY QUESTIONS

1. God's choice of Abraham to be the father of a great nation demonstrated what truth? _____

   _____

   _____

   _____

2. What power is given to the congregation of Yeshua alone in Scripture? _____

   _____

   _____

3. The believers in Acts 2:42-47 devoted themselves to what basic involvements? _____

   _____

   _____

   _____

4. What is a destructive attitude found in some believers today and why? _____

   _____

   _____

   _____

5. Why is it such a terrible offense to hurt or destroy a local body of believers? _____

_____

_____

6. What are God's main purposes for which we should be dedi-

cated to build the local congregation? _____

_____

_____

VERSES FOR MEMORIZATION

Hebrews 10:24-25
John 17:21-23
Acts 2:42-47
I Corinthians 3:16

Aa.—SIGNS AND ORDINANCES OF THE NEW COVENANT

In the plan of this Discipleship Book, we desire to have each local congregation separately instruct each believer in their practice of the signs or ordinances of the New Covenant. However, a few words on this important subject are in order. Hopefully, disciples will be carefully instructed in ways consistent with local practice.

Immersion and the application of water for cleaning symbolically were significant and prominant parts of ancient Judaism. John the Baptist (Immerser) applied the practice of immersing in water as an act of repentance and cleansing before God. This was to prepare for the coming of the Messiah. Yeshua applied the use of water for new believers. The meaning of cleansing and repentance were not lost. However, new meanings were added to the practice. First of all, the mikvah (cleansing bath) now became reflective of God's work in the circumcision of the heart (Colossians 2:11,12), our co-death and resurrection in identity with the Messiah (Romans 6:1-10), and our entrance into the body of believers (I Corinthians 10:1-4; 12:13). J. Danielou* points out significant evidence that among early Jewish believers the practice through prayer and faith was considered effective in deliverance from demonic oppression. Hence, fasting could often take place before the practice of the mikvah in Yeshua's name. It is crucial to understand that this is *the* ordinance of public profession of faith and entrance into the body in a recognized way. Furthermore, in faith obedience to the command, God's power in us through the Messiah's atonement and resurrection is made greater in our lives. Public confession of God's work and obedience in faith increase our spiritual life (Matthew 28:19, Acts 2:38).

As the mikvah in Yeshua's name is the ordinance of initiation into the body and into the power of his atonement and resurrection in us, so the Messiah's Supper is an act of renewing the power of Messiah's life in us as we remember His death for us. Originally instituted in the Passover Seder, Yeshua made the broken bread and wine to stand for His broken body and

---

* *The Theology of Jewish Christianity.*

shed blood for our sin. (Matthew 26:26-30, Luke 22:7-22). Partaking in faith places us in such a relationship with the Holy Spirit that He renews the power of Yeshua's atoning death and resurrection in us. The breaking of bread and the drinking of wine in remembrance of Yeshua is practiced by many beyond only the time of Passover. This was already the case in the New Testament (I Corinthians 11:7-34). The reality of the power of God in the context of celebrating the Messiah's Supper causes life in those who sincerely and in repentance partake in faith, but sickness and death in the insincere (I Corinthians 11:27-32). Participation in this ordinance is an important part of our ongoing faith relationship with God. However, it is only for those who examine themselves and confess and seek to turn from their sins (I Corinthians 11:27-28).

SECTION B—GIFTS AND MINISTRIES

The Bible teaches we are to build one another in the body through the anointing of the Spirit. The Holy Spirit (Ruach ha Kodesh) gives every believer gifts which are to be used to build the body. *Romans 12 and I Corinthians 12-14* provide us with essential information concerning the gifts of the Spirit. In addition, *Ephesians 4:11ff* outlines foundational gift ministries which are crucial to a proper understanding of the functioning of the body. The gifts of the Spirit may be given in ways which coordinate with the abilities, proclivities and other aspects of individual personality. However, the gifts are supernatural manifestations of the Spirit's anointing and not merely natural talents.

First let's look at the foundational gift ministries in Ephesians 4. We read in verse seven that when the Messiah ascended He gave gifts to men. He gave five foundational gift ministries,

> "to prepare God's people for works of service, so that the body of Messiah may be built up until we all reach unity in the faith and in the knowledge of the Son of God and become mature, attaining to the whole measure of the fullness of Messiah.
> "Then we will no longer be infants, tossed back and forth by the waves, and blown here and there by

every wind of teaching and by the cunning and craftiness of men in their deceitful scheming. Instead, speaking the truth in love, we will in all things grow up into Him who is the head, that is, Messiah. From Him the whole body, joined and held together by every supporting ligament, grows and builds itself up in love as each part does its work." (Ephesians 4:12-16)

Before we get into the details of the foundational gift ministries, we need to have a clear sense of their purpose as a whole. Their purpose is to *equip* the members of the body to do the *work of ministry*. All are to do the work of ministry. The congregation is not a group of spectators watching a group of leaders who are the actors. *Everyone* is to be engaged in service. Only by flowing with foundational ministries under the authority of the body, does maturity come about both in the individuals and in the congregation as a whole.

The purpose of the foundational gift ministries, outlined in verses 12 and 13, is that the body of Messiah be built up until we reach *unity in the faith* and in the knowledge of the Son of God. This is maturity, experiencing the fullness of Messiah. We become like Him and He is manifest in us.

To forsake God's provision of growth under foundational ministries is to continue in immaturity, or infancy. Such a person will be tossed about by every "wind of teaching," unstable, unreliable, and unfruitful. But by attending to body life under foundational gift ministries, we are to grow up into Him who is the head, Messiah.

The picture of the body of believers in Ephesians 4:16 is truly glorious. The community is to be *knit together*, joined and held together by supporting ligaments (foundational ministries under Yeshua's power), growing and building itself up in love, *as each part does its work*. What an image and goal for our commitment! God does not desire a bunch of separate bones and limbs which do their own separate thing. He wants an organized organism that functions in harmonized unity under leadership which hears from God.

We are now ready to look at the foundational ministries which are so important. They are those of apostles, prophets, evangelists, pastors, and teachers.

An apostle is one *sent out to plant and/or strengthen local congregations.* He is given special anointing of the Spirit for this purpose. Although his ministry comes with great authority, there are several misunderstandings to avoid. Today's apostles operate as the original apostles. However, their work builds on the foundations of these eyewitness apostles. The eyewitness apostles were the foundational teachers who gave us the Scriptures. They cannot be superseded, so all later teaching and ministry must be judged and tested by the Scriptures.

In addition, it is up to each local elder authority as to whether or not they will receive a person as having an apostolic ministry to them. The New Testament admonishes us to guard against receiving false apostles whose teaching is not in accord with the sound doctrine already laid out (Galatians 1).

Elders of the local body must guard the flock and judge all teaching, although before a recognized apostle there should be a submitted, learning spirit. The apostle as a congregational planter and upbuilder may move in several gift areas: miracles, prophecy, teaching, word of knowledge, and word of wisdom. The Apostle Paul moved in all of these areas in his ministry.

Messianic Jews particularly need to pray that this crucial ministry be established among them, so new congregations will be planted and existing ones strengthened.

An apostle is usually based in a local fellowship and may receive support from this congregation. However, his ministry is translocal. He needs relationships with others to whom he is accountable, because none of us ever outgrows his need for correction in relationships of mutual love and fellowship. Messianic Jews need not only pray for apostles to be raised up among them, but to hear from apostles given to the non-Jewish segments of the body as well. In New Testament times, a missionary was simply one with an apostolic mission to plant congregations. The word "missionary" and "apostle" are in part synonymous.

The second foundational gift ministry is that of a prophet. A prophet proclaims God's will supernaturally. He may bring a word which reveals sin, exhorts, applies the Word, predicts, or gives direction. The prophet's message and life must always be rigorously tested by Scripture (Deuteronomy 13:18, I Corinthians 14). Many have gone astray yielding to false prophets who contradict the written Word. Only after a person has shown stability of character and a consistently biblical prophetic gift can he or she attain to this position. This gift is extremely helpful in building up the body.

An evangelist is one who has a primary ministry of proclaiming the Good News to the lost. We are all called to be witnesses, but not all called to be evangelists. The evangelist has a ministry which includes an unusual ability for preaching and winning the lost, with the desire to orient one's entire life around it. An evangelist often spurs others to more effective witness. We can readily see the foundational nature of this gift. An evangelist is based in a local body but many have a translocal ministry.

A pastor or shepherd is one who cares for the local flock. The shepherd brings back sheep who have gone astray. He exhorts, corrects, counsels, prays and loves people into the likeness of the Messiah. The shepherds make up the elders in a congregation (I Peter 5, Hebrews 13:7,17). It is crucial that members and shepherds both seek to cultivate significant relationships with each other. Shepherds move in the gifts of *teaching, exhortation, healing, and mercy, and other areas.* I Timothy 3:1-7 gives the qualifications of a shepherd. The shepherd has a modeling role for others in family life, character, and zeal for the things of the Lord.

Teachers are crucial gift-ministers to the body. They explain the Word with a deep concern for accuracy. Teachers of all ages are important in enabling the body of believers to understand the Word better so they can live their lives in accordance with God's will.

May God enable us to recognize the foundational gift ministries which He has raised up and will raise up in our midst. May we come to the knowledge of the full maturity of the Messiah carefully making use of God's means for doing so in the body.

In addition to foundational gift ministries, *every believer has a primary ministry gift and can move in many gift manifestations.* Romans 12 lists seven primary gift ministries. Although it may not be an exhaustive list, most believers find themselves in one category or another. *If we are to serve God effectively it is crucial that we order our service to the body around the gift ministry God has given us.*

The limits of this discipleship program preclude a thorough discussion of ministry gifts. However, clarity concerning one's gifts should be worked out prayerfully with the confirmation of other believers and leaders. Some people teach that everyone has one primary gift ministry, even though they may move in other areas of the gifts. This is called the motivational gift.

Romans 12:1,2 is the introduction to these gifts. It calls for every believer to give his life as a living sacrifice to the Lord and to one another. We are to have a balanced evaluation of our place in the body, not a highly exalted vision. In Romans 12:4 we read:

> "Just as each of us has one body with many members, and these members do not all have the same function, so in Messiah *we who are many form one body*, and *each member belongs to all the others.* We have different gifts, according to the grace given us. If a man's gift is *prophesying*, let him use it in proportion to his faith. If it is *serving*, let him serve; if it is *teaching*, let him teach; if it is *encouraging*, let him encourage; if it is *contributing* to the needs of others, let him give generously; if it is leadership *(rulership-administration)*, let him govern diligently; if it is *showing mercy*, let him do it cheerfully."

The gift of prophesying is a motivation to declare God's message to the community. A person with prophetic motive desires to speak God's Word to reprove, correct, reveal sin, give specific application of the Word to the gathered community, and to give specific direction to the body. This gift is exercised in major public meetings as well as in smaller group and individual contexts. It is important that this gift be rigorously tested by the written Word and by other mature spiritually discerning people in the congregation.

A person recognizes this gift by a sensitivity to the Spirit regularly prompting him or her to speak to the body in various ways. There is also tremendous motivation to speak out and see true repentance and clear direction from God.

Often, a person with powerful prophetic gifts must guard against pride and impatience which become a negative attitude. The latter comes from expecting immediate results from the prophetic word rather than patiently praying through to results. Pride forgets the gift is unmerited and that all glory goes to the Lord.

A serving motivation involves a person in helping others with many projects of value to the body. These projects range from serving the congregation as a whole in areas of building and ground maintenance, mailings, committee tasks, and outreach, to giving one's self to individuals in the congregation who need help. The serving gift is one of the most crucial to the operation of the body. The supernatural anointing for this gift is as great as for any other gift. All in the body are to manifest serving, but not all have this as their primary motivational gift.

Serving is probably one of the most common ministry gifts given by the Spirit. However, pride causes many people not to recognize this gift in themselves. They desire a more glorious public ministry or else no ministry at all. Yet such a person usually finds when they do involve themselves in serving they feel fulfilled. How the body is hurt by this kind of pride. This is why Paul called for a proper evaluation in humility.

The serving gift is crucial for the functioning of many areas of the congregation. But there are dangers to be avoided in the serving personality. First of all, the servant person often expects everyone to have the same serving motive as himself. He gets discouraged seeing others doing less, and eventually, because he has taken his eyes off the Lord and focused on man, he ceases to walk in the power of the Spirit in faith. Pride is also a danger for the servant who is not given recognition for his work. It is well for others to give us recognition, but we are to "do it (serving) heartily unto the Lord," knowing our reward is in Him. We are not to grow "weary in well-doing" (Galatians 6:9).

The servant should also seek a steady level of prayed-out commitment in the Spirit. This helps him avoid pendulum swings between overextending himself and totally pulling back after getting burned out. A service-motivated person finds joy in seeing tasks accomplished before the Lord.

The teacher is one who loves the study and discovery of biblical truth. He is careful to handle the Word with accuracy. A person with a teaching motivation always wants to see others interested in study and learning. He loves to see the Word systematically and clearly presented and his heart rejoices in *truth made manifest.* Harmonizing various dimensions of biblical teaching also brings great joy to him.

The exhorter or encourager is both enabled to give counsel and direction to others and to encourage them by instilling hope. Some preachers are motivated more by teaching, some more by exhortation. A person with a gift of exhortation desires to motivate others to do what is right and to encourage them when they flag in zeal and faith. At times the exhorter seems lacking in the ability to listen and empathize adequately. He or she seems caught up in getting the individual or group on track and moving in accordance with God's program and purpose. He has to guard against being too pushy and too directive.

At times the exhorter can wear himself out in exhorting and needs exhortation himself. The exhorter is crucial in body life because he helps others get on track and begin functioning for the Lord. The exhortation gift may be publicly expressed in messages to the gathered community or in private counseling. But always exhortation must be given in love.

Contributing generously is the fifth gift in the list. Generosity is, of course, to be a characteristic of all believers. However, a generous person is one who truly desires to give of his money and possessions for the needs of others in the body, as well as to the body as a whole. Although everyone may give, the person with a generosity motive truly enjoys picking up the tab. There is an expansive attitude toward money; you can't outgive God and He will prosper those who are generous. And sure enough, the generous person eventually prospers. We have seen this gift in several members. Once a man who was almost bankrupt sought to give even though he did not have. He had to be restrained. Another loved to take others out and share joy with them. This was a regular occurrence. He had to be counseled to provide for his family and not give all away including both money and possessions. However, others with control have given to establish others in business, to fund facilities and to do great things for God.

The person of generosity loves to be able to identify areas and projects he can give to. He can be a great encouragement toward others giving generously. However, *the generous person needs wisdom so he can give to that which is of true worth.* If he lacks this wisdom it is well that he seek to confirm his giving with those who have wisdom. Also he must not forget to tithe to his own congregation.

Rulership or administration is the sixth gift area on the list. People with these gifts may serve as elders if they have other requisite gifts, or may serve on other boards, committees or coordinator positions in the congregation. They enjoy seeing a smooth running system of operation and are willing to give themselves in leadership to bring it about. They bring unity and harmonious relationship among the functions of the body. People with this gift are able to delegate, organize, and motivate.

The danger to a person who has this ministry is that he may in pride evaluate his leadership to be beyond further growth. Furthermore, governing in the body is a servant role. We are to govern so as to facilitate others in their ministries. The leader hears from the Lord, but must also be open to the Lord speaking through others. He must eschew a domineering way of leadership while being firm about his convictions.

The last gift mentioned is *showing mercy.* Praise God for this important gift. The person with this gift empathizes with all kinds of pain, mental and physical. He or she feels great compassion for those in need. They find it easier to "weep with those who weep" as Scripture enjoins (Romans 12:15). Yet they are hurt if their mercy is abused by hypocrisy and by people seeking to use them selfishly.

The person with the gift of mercy is drawn to the sick, the oppressed, and the poor. They offer hot soup to the needy and comfort to the aged. But the person with the gift of mercy should avoid the danger of offering mercy without wisdom. If he or she lacks wisdom, the help of others is important in their rightly exercising this gift. They also need to recognize that sometimes love's medicine is tough and requires discipline rather than "merciful" indulging (Romans 11:22). Mercy wrongfully applied is harmful. Often a person with the gift of mercy judges a prophet or exhorter as harsh. However, mercy and exhortation need each other to provide proper balance in the body.

In I Corinthians 12 we find another list of the gifts of the Spirit in terms of manifestations of the Spirit for the common good.

(It would be good for the student to read all of I Corinthians 12-14 to understand the orderly functioning of the body. In this section we can only briefly note the various manifestations and Paul's advice concerning them in this portion of Scripture.)

There is one body and one Spirit who is the source of all supernatural gift manifestations (I Corinthians 12:7). Believers are not to devalue each others' gifts nor are they to have pride over any particular gift. Every part of the body and every gift is necessary.

Although a person has a primary motivation gift, he may manifest many of the manifestations in I Corinthians 13. A person with a teaching motive may also distinguish spirits. A person who is an apostle may have the motive gift of teaching while at the same time demonstrating healing and prophecy as part of his total ministry. A person who serves may prophesy. All gifts are given by the Spirit and it is possible in any service that any committed believer may hear from the Lord for the body.

The manifestation gifts given in I Corinthians 12:7-11 are listed and briefly described here:

1. *The message of wisdom*—This is a Word from the Spirit giving practical guidance, a solution, or a deepening of understanding. It may be manifest in a public service or in private. It is very helpful in counseling. It may be delivered simply when a person shares his advice or understanding for the body.
2. *The message of knowledge*—This is a Word of the Spirit giving supernatural knowledge of a situation or event. It is also helpful in counsel and leadership. God may reveal

the root of sin to a counselor or give knowledge of an unrevealed problem in the body. Knowledge reveals the facts and wisdom reveals how to deal with the facts, the situation being what it is (e.g., John 4—Yeshua with woman at the well).

3. *Faith*—This is the manifestation of believing in the Spirit for specific promises in the Word or in the Spirit. Although everyone exercises faith, this gift manifestation is a prominent measure of faith given for the whole body which encourages others to faith.

4. *Miraculous power* confirms God's presence and power so as to turn others to the Lord. Miraculous power does not necessarily confirm all that is taught. Teaching should come from teachers. Often a person with miraculous power is assumed to have wisdom and teaching, and poor doctrine results from this.

5. *Prophecy* is speaking out in the Spirit for the Lord, giving correction, prediction, direction, and comfort.

6. *Discernment* of spirits is crucial in recognizing the nature of and presence of evil spirits. It is very helpful in the ministry of deliverance from them because it aids in the diagnosis of a person's problem.

7. *Speaking in tongues* here is not the devotional use of tongues spoken of in I Corinthians 14:4, which is edifying though not understood. It is rather a speaking out in unlearned syllables as a spur to an interpretation or as a catalyst for an interpretation. It may sound more or less like a real language, but it may be more an intuitive expression of the emotion or feeling of God which will come forth in the message.

8. *Interpretation of tongues* is to be judged as prophecy.

I Corinthians 14 gives crucial instruction concerning manifestations. First of all, "The spirits of prophets are subject to the control of prophets." (verse 32). The parts of a worship service in which there are public manifestations are to be done in an orderly way for the strengthening of the body (verse 26). One person is to speak at a time, whether it be with a message, a hymn, a word of wisdom, or a Scripture. In addition, after a message in tongues is given and there is no interpretation, the person is to be told their gift is private and they are mistakenly using it in public. There must be order (I Corinthians 14:33,40).

There is a glorious dimension of the Spirit which orchestrates a service both by elements planned ahead of time by the leaders who are led by the Spirit, and in periods of unplanned manifestations. A choir may sing an anthem to the Lord and a prophecy may be given to His glory, but we are commanded to seriously consider and weigh all prophetic manifestations and "prove that which is good" (I Thessalonians 5:21) under elder oversight (I Corinthians 14:29).

It is a great joy when a worship service harmonizes in the Spirit and planned songs and messages from gift manifestations blend wonderfully with the preached Word. This is a glorious joy in the body.

A few words should be mentioned here about pride. If there is to be freedom in the Spirit we must realize there will be times when people speak out in immaturity, or without clarity, or even carnally. Error must be disavowed, but if we are too hard on those who are imperfect, we will instill fear in the body and stifle true manifestations. If there is a repeated problem we should privately speak to the one involved. Pride, however, prefers to lose the manifestation rather than put up with the embarrassment of mistakes. We reject this.

There are three responses to public manifestation. There is the "Amen, we affirm it." There is also the response where the body lets it pass with no real acceptance or disavowal. But when there is error, it is important the leaders say, "We are sorry, brother or sister, but we cannot receive this word. Please speak to us (the elders or a representative of the elders) afterward."

There are times in a service when the congregation engages in free spontaneous praise. Some speak in tongues, others mumble praises in Hebrew and English, but all have their minds focused on the Lord. Legalists have accused groups of violating Scripture in allowing more than one person to speak at a time. However, we believe this is a manifestation of the Scriptural principle. This principle, read in context, is seeking to keep people from talking on top of one another when a message is being given to be heard. Confusion is to be avoided. However, when we say, "Let's each praise the Lord," there is no confusion. Everyone knows they are each to praise the Lord and not try to listen to others.

I Corinthians 13 is the chapter which puts the gifts of the Spirit in context. The Corinthians eagerly desired gifts of greater prominence, but Paul told them, "But eagerly desire the greater gifts. And now I will show the most excellent way." (v.31).

This better way is the way of love, giving sacrificial love that seeks not its own way or glory. If our ultimate motivation is love we will only desire those gifts needed for the good of the body (I Corinthians 14:12). We won't care which gift we are given as long as the needed gifts are given and used for the good of the body.

(The student should read I Corinthians 13 at this point.)

May God give you this great love for the body.

STUDY QUESTIONS

1. Name and define the foundational gift ministries listed in Ephesians 4:11ff.

   a. _____

   _____

   b. _____

   _____

   c. _____

   _____

   d. _____

   _____

e. _____

_____

2. Name and define the seven primary ministry (motivational gifts) in Romans 12.

a. _____

_____

_____

b. _____

_____

_____

c. _____

_____

_____

d. _____

_____

_____

e. _____

_____

_____

f. _____

_____

_____

g.   _____

_____

_____

3. Explain how a person may move in the Spirit in several gift
   manifestations while still having one primary gift ministry.

_____

_____

_____

_____

_____

SECTION C—THE MARKS OF THE BODY

Today, in distinction from past ages, the follower of Yeshua is confronted with a tremendous variety of religious organizations, Bible studies, men's and women's organizations, clubs, outreach organizations, and other such groups. Many of these organizations merit our prayerful support, but some do not. Some people confuse a commitment to these groups with a commitment to Yeshua's body. Only a commitment to a true local expression of the body of believers fulfills the biblically revealed will of God and it must take precedence over all other commitments.

How do we recognize that local body? There are several identifying marks. If any of these marks is missing, a group is not really a true New Testament congregation. Here are the identifying marks:

1. The group considers itself to be a local expression of the body or a full-fledged congregation. The size of the group is not significant in determining this.
2. The group meets regularly for worship, praise, and the teaching of the Word as a community (Hebrews 10:24).
3. The group celebrates the bread and the wine of the Messiah's supper (I Corinthians 11) and the Mikvah (immersion) or baptism of new believers.
4. The group has recognized elder-leadership and considers itself submitted to their authority under the authority of the Bible (I Timothy 3 and I Peter 5:2).
5. The group's foundation is the Messiah rather than business commitments, hobbies, or other involvements which might draw believers together (Ephesians 2:20, I Corinthians 3:11).

In this section we will elaborate on some of these marks. The fourth identifying mark, however, is the topic of the next chapter. At the close of this section is a discussion of the general calling of each member of the body in regards to four central biblical teachings: staying close to one another, supporting one another financially, serving one another in practicing hospitality, and submitting lovingly to one another.

If a group is confused about its identity, as to whether it is or is not either a full-fledged congregation or seeking to be one, it certainly cannot fulfill its purpose. Where there is no vision, the people perish. Faith requires a perception in the Spirit of who we are and from this knowledge, what we are to be about.

Secondly, a true congregation gathers for praise, worship, and the teaching of the Word. In many places, Messianic Jews have rediscovered the life and joy which characterized biblical praise and worship. Although we do not seek to absolutize any particular form of biblical worship, there are several things to note.

Some see worship as a reflection of the tabernacle of David (II Samuel 6) in which praise was sung to God. Yeshua said the Father seeks true worshipers who will worship Him in Spirit and in truth (John 4:23,24). The freedom in praise in Scripture includes spontaneity, dance, raising hands, and written prayers which are chanted (the book of Psalms includes material which was chanted).

Such freedom in praise delights the Lord and brings His presence. It lifts us out of our self-centered concerns into the joy of God. Praise and freedom also greatly offend the fleshly and proudly-reserved. Scripture teaches decency and order, but the freedom for praise and even mistakes in worship are much greater than the proud will allow. Praise and worship in the gathered community is akin to entering the Holy of Holies. When entered into by faith it renews us in Spirit. It is helpful to note the amazing variety of worship expressions in Scripture:

* *audible voice*—Psalm 66:1,8,17; 98:4; Acts 16:25
* *shouting*—Psalm 47:1; 35:27; 132:9,16
* *singing*—Psalm 47:6; I Corinthians 14:26; Colossians 3:16
* *speaking in tongues*—Acts 2:11; 10:46; I Corinthians 14:2
* *laughter*—Psalm 126:1-3; 63:3-5
* *musical instruments*—Psalm 33:1-3; 150:1-6
* *clapping hands*—Psalm 47:1, 98:4-8; Isaiah 55:12
* *amens*—Nehemiah 5:13; 8:16; Psalm 89:52; 106:48
* *lifting hands*—Psalm 63:4; 28:2; 88:9

* *dancing*—Psalm 150:4; 89:15; 30:11,12; 149:2,3
* *bowing and kneeling*—Psalm 95:6; Ephesians 3:14; Nehemiah 8:6
* *choirs*—II Chronicles 20:21,22; Nehemiah 11:23
* *hymns and chanted prayers*—Ephesians 5:19,20; Luke 1:46,55

When we come to worship we are to primarily seek to exalt God and His Messiah. This is to be our concentration. *We seek to worship in unity as a body while at the same time not being offended by paying too much attention to those around us.* If someone repeatedly jolts others out of worship, we should correct them in love. It is also helpful to note some Hebrew words for praise and worship; to get a full sense of the variety God gives us.

* *Yadah*—the extended hand, to worship with extended hands.
* *Tovah*—to extend the hands in adoration or offering.
* *Italal*—to cast up, extol, shine, boast, rave, celebrate.
* *Shabbach*—to address in a loud tone, triumph, glory (Psalm 117:1; 63:1,3,4—"My lips shall praise (shabbach) Thee.").
* *Burach*—to kneel, to bless God in adoration, to bow receptively.
* *Zamar*—to touch the strings.
* *T'villah*—to sing or praise with songs of the Spirit, at time unprepared.

We have found in a Jewish context a wonderful blend of form and freedom. Great songs and psalms from the Jewish heritage provide touchstones for spontaneous prayer and praise.

There is an illustration which gives a mental picture of progressing into praise in the worship service. When we gather together it is like going up to the ancient Temple to meet God in the Holy of Holies. On the way to the Temple as the people ascended the mount, they prepared with dance and songs of celebration called psalms of ascent. The atmosphere became quieter in the inner court. The high priest alone entered the

Holy of Holies in great reverence and quietness. When the people descended the mount, there were also songs of faith and celebration.

This is how we compare our worship to our Jewish heritage. There are songs of celebration, exuberant praise, and also quiet times when we recall these verses: "Be still and know that I am God," for the "Lord is in His holy temple, let all the earth keep silent before Him."

It is in such silence that we hear Him speak to us, at times through other members in our midst. Singing the shema has become an expression of commitment while still in the Holy of Holies part of our worship.

If you would worship God truly, with *kavvanah* (true heart intent), according to the reverence which is due Him, come to services on time. Do not barge into the Holy of Holies (I Corinthians 3:16), but prepare yourself in prayer during the early portions of the service. Lateness and other lazy traits reveal a poor attitude and blunt the fullness of the presence of the Spirit which God would pour out on us in worship. Flow with the Spirit and with the body without distraction and gain a sense of the whole drift of the service. Seek to hear God and be renewed as you praise Him. Messianic Jewish worship is a unique experience. The body gathered for worship is the Lord's temple (I Corinthians 3:16).

The service of worship and praise both prepares us to hear God's Word and respond to it. The preached Word is central to the life of the body. Although it is possible and worthwhile to purchase tapes by the greatest teachers, we must realize the teaching ministry in our own local body is the most crucial for our lives. This is because the leaders of our local assembly seek to hear from the Lord what He would say at a particular time. Through being taught together as a body and thus sharing the same experience as a congregation in the Lord's timing, we grow together in unity at the proper pace. The atmosphere of commitment in the local body enables us to receive the Word in the depths of our being so it produces fruit. Faith is our response and it brings healing to body, soul, and spirit.

Thirdly, the regular practice of the Messiah's supper and the Mikvah in Yeshua, called "baptism," is also a mark of a true congregation.

The Mikvah is the ceremony of initiation into the body of believers. Through it we publicly confess our faith in the Messiah Yeshua. Specifically, the act professes that we have died with the Messiah and have risen with Him (Romans 6), and that we have received the circumcision of the heart (Colossians 2:11-13). Originally the Mikvah was a Jewish ceremony of cleansing especially used for a person converting to Judaism.

The Mikvah in Yeshua is commanded in Matthew 28:10 and Acts 2:38. The confession of our faith publicly enables us to receive fully the work of God which is ours in Yeshua (Romans 10:9,10). In the early community of believers, the Mikvah was an act approached with repentance along with the faith there would be deliverance from oppression through this public act.

The Messiah's supper is the celebration of the gathered community which renews the power of Yeshua's atoning death in us. At the Passover Seder just before His death, Yeshua instituted this memorial and used the elements of bread and wine to symbolize His broken body and shed blood (see I Corinthians 11:23-26). We should try to be present whenever the congregation celebrates the Messiah's supper. When we receive the bread and wine, by faith, we receive the renewal of His atoning life anew. This special renewal strengthens us in the most wonderful spiritual sense.

However, we would be amiss if we did not mention the warning given in I Corinthians 11 by Paul. This meal only strengthens those who partake of it in true sincerity. These are people who:

1. are sincerely repentant of sin and expect to run from it. For them it strengthens their resolve and ability to overcome sin.
2. discern the body (I Corinthians 11:29). When the elements are celebrated, we are the body of the Lord and the elements represent His body given for us. To partake without due reverence is a serious sin before God. This is why we read:

   "A man ought to examine himself before he eats of the bread and drinks of the cup. For anyone who eats and drinks without recognizing the body of the Lord eats and drinks judgement on himself. That is why many among you are weak and sick, and a number of you have fallen asleep." (I Corinthians 11:28-30)

But partaken of in true repentance and faith, what a glorious meal, what a joyous, solemn celebration.

Every member of the body is called to a body-life-commitment. As stated earlier in this section, Scripture lays out four primary commitments to a fulfilled life together in the body. They are: staying close to one another, supporting one another financially, serving one another in practicing hospitality, and submitting lovingly to one another.

In Acts 2:46 we are told about that glorious first community in Jerusalem, that day by day they "broke bread in their homes and ate together with glad and sincere hearts." To break bread in another person's home was the deepest experience of acceptance. This passage is an image of fellowship, an intimate care and sharing based on our common faith in the Lord. Scripture calls upon us to uphold one another, to correct one another, to rejoice with those who rejoice and weep with those who weep, bearing one another's burdens in love (Galatians 6:1,2).

It is only in loving involvement with each other that we truly pattern the life of Yeshua. All who are in Yeshua are our brothers and sisters, and we are our brother's keepers; we are responsible for each other. This means giving ourselves beyond personal friendships to those who do not seem to have yet developed beautiful personalities in the Lord. In this regard, Scripture enjoins us not to show partiality (James 2:1) and to practice hospitality. We read:

"Above all, love each other deeply, because love covers over a multitude of sins. Offer hospitality to one another without grumbling." (I Peter 4:8,9)

Practicing hospitality includes:

1. Opening our homes *regularly for fellowship with other believers.* This includes personal friends, but is espe-

cially related to new-comers in our congregation as well as others. Hospitality should be *exercised frequently.* Why not even try an open house?

2. Opening our homes for those who are visiting from out-of-town. We can double up in bedrooms. This includes putting people up who are moving into our community before they find new housing. Our homes belong to God. We are only stewards.

We should be open to share needs, not give easy pat answers, and be willing to pray for one another. Staying close to one another includes a decision to order one's life around the community of one's call. Living near one another and finding careers which dovetail with the call to a local congregation is part of staying close to one another. We are an extended family in Yeshua. We must live like it!

Supporting one another financially begins with the principle of the tithe. In the Old Testament period, the Israelites gave one-tenth of their material possessions to support the priests and Levites who ministered to the whole community. In the power of the Spirit under God's grace, we are enabled to do much more. But we should at least not rob God of the tenth which is used to support the ministry of our extended family.

When we tithe, the floodgates of blessing open to us. We acknowledge that all we have is God's and we are only stewards. When we do not tithe we show lack of faith, which closes the gates of God's blessing, and brings unforeseen financial plagues.

"But you ask, 'How do we rob You?'

"In tithes and offerings. You are under a curse—the whole nation of you—because you are robbing Me. Bring the whole tithe into the storehouse . . . Test me in this and see if I will not throw open the floodgates of heaven and pour out so much blessing that you will not have room enough for it." (Malachi 3:8-10)

The New Testament exhorts the same principle of giving in Luke 6:38 and expects even more under the power of God's Spirit in us. We are not to give because of the return we will gain, but out of love and faith. Love and faith produce an abundance in which God meets all our needs (Philippians 4:19). The work of the congregation depends on sustained consistent giving rather than sporadic whims. Beyond our tithe, we should pray for the Spirit's leading about additional giving to the congregation and other ministries.

Some have asked if the tithe should be given outside the congregation. Larry Tomczak of Silver Spring Christian Community in suburban Washington D.C., responds to this in his usual plain and profound way by saying, "This would be like going to McDonald's and being served a large meal, and then paying for it at Burger King." The community as a whole may give to other ministries, but to divide our tithe (the first 10%) is like paying another family's bills instead of our own. It shows lack of mutual submission to one another.

In addition, the community should seek to meet the financial needs of all its members whose financial difficulties are not due to laziness or clearly manifested sin patterns of which there is no repentance. We are one in the Messiah. We must act accordingly.

We are called to submit lovingly one to another (Ephesians 5:21). Beyond the issues of leadership and authority which are taken up in the next chapter, we want to say a word on the mutual submission which should characterize all of us. To submit one to another means to put the other's needs above your own, to try to stand in the shoes of the other person and defer to one another's desires if there is no moral impropriety in doing so. This is the way of true love and avoiding conflict.

Lastly, we are called to serve one another practically, showing ourselves to be "servants of one another." Can we share with those who are sick or who need our help in chores? This includes child care, home repair, transportation help, and scores of other practical ways of helping and working together.

Some people ask how to decide upon which community to become a part of. We would encourage you to seek a place where you sense the peace of *the Spirit in the sense of God's call* to you. *The issue is not how perfect a body is or how great the preacher is, but where you are needed and called to build.* The congregation which has reached out to you and through whose members you came to the Lord, or through whom you have been discipled, is usually the place of your calling. You need one congregation of commitment or you will become awfully confused. Of course, for a Messianic Jew there are aspects of Jewish calling which have bearing on the choice of his or her commitment.

May God bless you as you find the joy of a place in the local community of faith!

STUDY QUESTIONS

1. Name five crucial marks for identifying a true biblical congregation as the place of your commitment.

   a. _____

   b. _____

   c. _____

   d. _____

   e. _____

2. How is our worship service similar to the ancient Israelites going up to the Temple to worship? _____

   _____

   _____

   _____

3. Define the meaning of the Mikvah in Yeshua and the Messiah's supper. _____

_____

_____

_____

4. How do we practice hospitality? _____

_____

_____

_____

5. Why should we tithe or give one-tenth of our income to the

   local body? _____

_____

_____

_____

VERSES FOR MEMORIZATION

I Peter 5:8,9
Galatians 6:1,2
John 4:23,24

AUTHORITY AND DISCIPLINE

VI. AUTHORITY AND DISCIPLINE

The question of authority engenders great controversy. There are several reasons for this. American culture breeds a separatist, autonomous concept of human life. "I am accountable to no one but myself." This attitude, which diametrically opposes Scripture, where *we are our brother's keeper.* (Genesis 4) has pervaded the lives of many believers. Secondly, many have reacted to cultic control and a tyranny of authority in immature religious groups. This reaction has been so severe among some people that they reject *the biblical teaching* on authority in the body. Thankfully, *the written Word* is our highest authority. In contrast, cultic authority seeks to destroy a person's conscience and thinking ability which results in a dependent immature person who requires the leader to be his conscience and brain.

Biblically enjoined authority corrects, disciplines, and counsels so as to develop a mature person with a sensitive, active conscience and ability to hear from the Lord. Ultimately, authority may give direction for the congregation and may counsel, but the individual must make his own final decisions and stand before God on his own. Authority may use dialogue and biblical texts for persuasion, but must never use psychological manipulation or immoral pressures to gain its ends. We appeal to the conscience with the Word and encourage the knowledge of the Word. The cult leader says, "Depend on me for knowledge and direction without question." But Scripture enjoins us to try all things and *prove* that which is good. Questioning on the basis of Scripture is proper if done in a positive attitude of love.

SECTION A—THE WORD AND AUTHORITY

The Bible is our highest authority for testing, teaching, and practice. It gives proper understanding of other levels of authority. The regular reading, memorization, and study of the Word and prayer are *the most essential elements* of a stable spiritual life. We read of the Word:

> "All Scripture is God-breathed and is useful for teaching, rebuking, correcting, training in righteousness, so that the man of God may be thoroughly equipped for every good work." (II Timothy 3:16)

All Scripture is a product of God's breathing it out. This is what "inspiration" means. God did not completely supersede the personalities of the biblical writers, but used their personalities to produce a product which stated just what He wanted stated. *Thus the Bible is totally true in the things any biblical writer claimed to teach by his words.* Its spiritual and moral teaching *trains us in righteousness* under the power of the Spirit. When we are trained in righteousness, we are equipped for every good work.

Peter put it a different way when he said, "For prophecy never had its origin in the will of man, but men spoke from God as they were carried along by the Holy Spirit." (II Peter 1:21). Another version puts it, "Holy men of God spake as they were moved by the Holy Spirit."

The Scriptural books provide us with poetry, letters, historical narrative, moral and legal instruction, predictive prophecy, and much more. Over 40 men authored the Bible over a 2,000 year period. The words of these 40 authors are inspired and the very words of God. This is why Yeshua could say that neither "the smallest letter, not the least stroke of a pen, will by any means disappear from the Law." (Matthew 5:18), and that "the Scripture cannot be broken." (John 10:35b). This amazing collection of writings we call the Bible has *these remarkable marks of God's authorship*:

1. It is consistent in its teachings on God, man, salvation, and morality.

2. In many passages it claims to be God's Word with, "Thus saith the Lord," and this is the commandment of God permeating its texts (I Corinthians 14:3).
3. Its prophetic predictions are coherent and historically accurate. The broad sweep of Israel's history and the rise and fall of many nations are accurately predicted.
4. Wherever archaeological discoveries relate to historic statements of the Bible, the Bible is seen to be compatible with these discoveries.
5. Our supreme teacher, Yeshua, taught the full truth of the Bible. His resurrection from the dead, attested to by uncontradicted first century testimony, authenticates all of His teaching. When Yeshua quoted Scripture, it was considered to settle the issue.

The books we have in our Bible are uniquely attested as the product of Israel's ancient prophets who were in a tradition of true faithfulness to God. Ancient Jewish testimony attests to the validity of all the books in the Tenach, which also make up the 39 books of the Protestant Old Testament. The New Testament books are the product of the original 12 witnesses and the other witnesses they accepted into their circle of authority (James, Paul, Jude, Luke). Godly believers have also confirmed in the Spirit the incomparable difference between the books we have in the Bible and other religious writings from biblical times.

The test of the inclusion of writings in our Bible is *prophetic or apostolic origins and the unified witness of the Spirit in the historic communities of faith, who received the books of the Bible and affirmed their inspiration and apostolic origin.* This is also the teaching of Ephesians 2:20 which affirms that the foundational teachings are from the prophets and the apostles. The Bible is the foundational teaching in written form, because we are "built on the *foundation of the apostles and prophets*, with Messiah Yeshua Himself as the chief cornerstone."

"Apostles," as used here, refers to the original foundational New Testament witnesses: the 12 disciples and their associates.

The Bible is a book in which God accommodates Himself to speak to people in the ordinary languages of human speech and writing. The Spirit of God gives insight into the Scripture and its application. However, the Scripture is also to be the *test* of what we think the Spirit is saying. That's why we read we are to test and approve God's will and to try all things and prove what is good (Romans 12, I Corinthians 14:20, I John 4:1). If the Bible is to be an objective test of the Spirit, it must be seen as a book with objective means of understanding it, as well as the subjective means of the Spirit.

Since the Bible is written in *human language, we can understand it according to:*

1. the rules of grammar of the original language,
2. the definitions of words in the language at the times of writing,
3. the cultural context of the times, the uses of words, phrases, and other blocks of material, whether parable, poetry, and so on, and
4. the context of the teaching of whole books. This especially must be taken into account to understand verses and smaller units in individual books.

These rules are the basis for translating the Bible into English from Hebrew and Greek, in which the Old and New Testaments respectively are written. However, a single word or two is often not adequate to fully understand the original word in Hebrew or Greek. This is why good commentaries, written by believing scholars, are helpful in giving an accurate expanded understanding of the original Hebrew and Greek. Every believer should respect the work of believing scholarship which gives us the gift of English Bibles and commentaries.

The Bible gives us important teaching on our relation to human authorities in this life. It describes both the limits and the spheres in which human authority operates. Our primary concern is authority in the body of believers, but it is important that we outline the other spheres as well. The Scripture outlines four spheres of authority: the family, the state, the congregation, and in a less clarified way, the work place.

In each sphere of life authorities are given. *In the family, parents are given authority for raising children; the state is*

given authority to insure justice and social stability; the con-
gregation is given authority for the teaching and discipline of its
members; and the employer is given authority to oversee
workers in his employ for contracted work.

Authorities in each sphere must understand the limits of
their authority as being only applicable in the spheres for
which they are appointed by God. If they overstep the boundaries of their proper sphere, they are not to be obeyed. "We must
obey God rather than men." (Acts 5:29).

Of course, whenever we must disobey God's constituted
authority we should do so without an attitude of rebellion and
with a submissive heart toward God. In these cases, it is well to
consider making an appeal to see if there is some other way to
satisfy authorities without violating Scriptural principles.

The family unit is the first sphere of authority found in
Scripture. In the family, parents are given authority for the
training, education, and spiritual nurture of their offspring
(Deuteronomy 6:4ff). The Bible places the husband as head of
the household, the servant-leader of the home. Leadership in
Scripture is not a role of domination but of facilitation. A wise
husband seeks accord and confirmation from his wife. A wise
wife submits to her husband within the boundaries of biblical
consistency, but gives *positive* input and criticism as well. (See
Ephesians 5:22-23.)

The husband-wife relationship parallels the relationship of
the Messiah and His people. The structure of authority in the
family must not be usurped by the state or the religious community. For example, parents are free to draw from the religious community and the state for the education of their children. However, the parents are ultimately responsible for their
children and must carefully weigh their use of resources. If the
state violates the parent's prerogative to decide the religious
and other educational directions of their child except where the
parents seek to instill crime (the state's prerogative is maintaining justice), then the state has overstepped its bounds of authority and must be resisted.

The state is ordained of God to maintain justice and civil
order (Romans 13). It is not to "bear the sword in vain" but is to
reward good and punish evil. Leaders who are grounded in

Scripture should understand the purpose and limits of their powers. Social programs must be defended on the basis of the basic purposes of government, or the state will grow too powerful and become a tyrant.

Revelations 13 gives a picture of the state overreaching its bounds and becoming a tyrant, demanding an allegiance and worship due only to God. But the believer is called to pray for his leaders, show a submissive attitude of cooperation to governmental authority, and only resist in faith when the state oversteps its bounds or does evil itself. The prophetic function of the biblical religious community is important in this regard.

Employer-employee relationships are the least spoken of in Scripture. Principles of employer-employee relationships can be found in Paul's comments on the slave/master relationship if proper qualifications are given (Ephesians 6:5-9). The authority of an employer is not a permanent authority. A person may be self-employed or switch jobs when contractual obligations end. Whenever a believer enters into contract he must always seek to honor his word. He must not engage in work which is immoral or illegal.

Employers must seek to fairly share profits and treat employees with respect. A contractual relationship of authority is part of the work situation between employees and superiors. Work should be done cooperatively under the direction of supervisors and done "heartily as unto the Lord." (Ephesians 6).

The body of believers is the authority sphere primarily spoken of in the New Covenant Scriptures. It is given the responsibility for the nurture, growth, discipline, and education of the believers in its midst. It also is given special power over the devil and his forces, the power to settle disputes between believers, and the imperative to reach the lost with the Good News of Yeshua the Messiah. God has a structure for authority in the body. This is the subject of the next sections.

STUDY QUESTIONS

1. Proper authority does not seek to produce an immature, dependent person; biblically enjoined authority seeks to

_____

_____

_____

2. When we speak of the Bible's inspiration according to II

   Timothy 3:16, we say all Scripture is a product of _____

_____

_____

The Bible is thus totally true in all _____

_____

3. List the marks which reflect that God is the author of Scripture:

   a. _____

   _____

   b. _____

   _____

   c. _____

   _____

   d. _____

_____

e. _____

_____

4. The books we accept as part of the Bible pass which tests for

   inclusion? _____

   _____

   _____

   _____

5. The Bible is an objective base for testing all teaching. To be
   an objective test there must be objective rules for interpreting it. We have listed four rules for interpretation. They are:

   a. _____

   b. _____

   c. _____

   d. _____

6. We have listed four spheres of authority in Scripture. List
   the four spheres, any references to Bible passages we spoke
   about, and a brief sentence describing the area given to the
   authorities in the four spheres.

   a. _____

   _____

   _____

   _____

b. _____

_____

_____

_____

c. _____

_____

_____

_____

d. _____

_____

_____

_____

VERSES FOR MEMORIZATION

Deuteronomy 6:4-9

SECTION B—THE BODY OF BELIEVERS, A THEOCRACY

The body of believers is a theocracy. It operates under the Lordship of its head, Yeshua the Messiah. Great misunderstanding and strife result when this fact is not understood. Many seek to impose an American, political, democratic model on the functioning of the body. This is bound to hinder the progress of God's congregation. In the Scripture, *authority in the local body is plural, functional, and charismatic.* We will explain what we mean by these terms.

First of all, Scripture represents the primary human authority of the body of believers to be vested in a plurality of elders. The congregational planter may appoint the first elders when men of adequate maturity make their appearance.

It says in Acts 14:23, "They appointed elders for them in each church." Again and again Scripture makes it clear that the body of elders is *given the anointing* to lead, shepherd and discipline. This is clear from several passages and the usages of terms in them.

For example, *"poimaino"* means to shepherd and is also translated rule or feed. It is used in John 21:16, Acts 20:28, I Corinthians 9:7 and in I Peter 5:2. Furthermore, we read of those *set over* or *at the head of* in I Thessalonians 5:12, I Timothy 3:4,5,12 and 5:17. We find a parallel in I Timothy 3:4,5, between a man being an adequate ruler of his family and ruling over a congregation, because "If anyone does not know how to manage his own family, how can he take care of God's church?"

I Peter 5 commands the elders (in the plural) to "be shepherds of God's flock that is under your care." Further reading of the New Testament shows that everywhere without exception there is clear evidence that congregations were to be ruled by leaders. For example:

> "Respect those who work hard among you, who are over you in the Lord and who admonish you." (I Thessalonians 5:12)

> "The elders who direct the affairs of the church well are worthy of double honor." (I Timothy 5:17)

"Remember your leaders, who spoke the Word of
God to you. . . and submit to their authority. . . greet
all your leaders . . ." (Hebrews 13:7,17,24)

The fact that elders were seen as ruling in plurality, even if
one person achieved leadership among the elders, is seen in
several passages where *elders as a group are regularly addressed
as the leaders of particular congregations:*

"Paul and Barnabas appointed elders for them in
each church. . . "(Acts 14:23)

"the Apostles and elders . . ." (Acts 15:2,4,6,22,23)

"all the elders were present . . ." (Acts 21:18)

"together with the overseers and deacons . . ."
(Philippians 1:1)

"He should call the elders of the church . . ."
(James 5:14)

In Acts 20, Paul called the elders of Ephesus to "Guard
yourselves and all the flock of which the Holy Spirit has made
you overseers. Be shepherds of the church of God. . . " The
word overseer or bishop is a synonym for elder. If we are
concerned as believers to obey the pattern of truth laid out in
Scripture, we should be concerned to be rightly related to the
leaders who are the shepherds of the flock.

The question, "Who are the elders to whom I am to look for
leadership and direction?" should be the concern of every
believer. There is no true relationship to body life without
being subject to leadership and flowing with it.

Secondly, we said *leadership is charismatic.* Ruling is one of
the gifts listed in Romans 12:6-8. According to Scripture, an
elder-servant-leader *is one who has the requisite gifts of the
Spirit to be able to carry on his task.* There are gifts of ruling,
counsel or teaching (I Timothy 3), and a loving heart for the
congregation and its individual members (I Corinthians 13).

Thirdly, and as a correlation of the above point, leadership is *functionally recognized. Other leaders appoint* those who are seen to already be functioning in a leadership role with respect from the people. People look to this person for advice, biblical knowledge, and healing love. The person is apt to go after stray sheep. In answer to the question, "How do you know who is an elder?"—a leader is one who is seen to be eldering by other leaders and members.

Various congregations have various means of recognizing these truths. In congregations I have led, the leadership has been respected in having the wisdom and caution to choose new elders for ordination. However, if a person is truly an elder, the people will also perceive it. That is why our congregation, Beth Messiah in Washington, D.C., requires affirmation by the congregation for a person to assume this role.

Because an elder may fall from adequacy of leadership, we require reaffirmation every three years. Other congregations do not have a formal affirmation by congregants, but take into account the congregational response to a person before appointment. It is true that congregations who elect that leadership democratically sometimes produce a good board of elders. But my experience has been that the democratic model of people running against each other for office produces many carnal results. People who lose elections are hurt and sometimes individuals are elected because of a winsome personality or a record of hard work, not because they are truly qualified as elders. Other elders may recognize the problem, but are powerless in a democratic model to do anything about it. Furthermore, we simply do not see the democratic model taught in Scripture.

Some Messianic congregations maintain a board of Shammashim which oversees finances, building, charitable endeavors and other matters, *in submission to the board of elders,* who have final say on decisions. Qualifications for Shammashim (deacons) are outlined in the book of Timothy (I Timothy 3).

Certainly our discussion up to this point raises several questions: What is the nature of elder authority? Over what areas does it extend? What are the limits of authority and submission? How am I to respond if a person in the role of eldership seems unqualified? The attempt to achieve biblically based answers to these questions occupies the rest of this section.

First of all, the purpose of the elders is to be helpful, to advise, and to correct. There is nothing, however, which gives the eldership the right to supersede an individual as a person who must stand before God in good conscience. The advice and counsel of an elder is *voluntarily sought* by members as a correlation of love.

A member is free to reject advice and counsel in areas which do not directly affect the functioning of the body. But members must be aware of pride and rebellion in their heart, which is symptomatized by constantly rejecting advice. Each member is also responsible to grow in the knowledge of the Word. He must never obey elder advice contrary to the Word, even if it means withdrawing from the body.

The eldership is instituted by God to coordinate the body. Thus it is the prerogative of the elders to set priorities, establish programs and ministries, allocate funds, and oversee the functioning of all activities. However, wise elders build the trust of their people by seeking input and feedback, and by disclosing what they are doing and why, when the matter is not related to private counseling situations.

The membership should seek to see the vision God is bringing forth from the leadership. Individuals can only walk in unity with the body if they share the vision and flow with the leadership. If they cannot do this there may be pride, rebellion, or other sins in their life, or perhaps they are in the wrong congregation.

The eldership is also charged by God to correct sin and even bar those from the congregation who are in serious error. Scripture states three sins for which a person must be expelled from the body of believers. One is gross immorality from which the person does not repent. Paul enjoined the congregation at Corinth to expel a man who lived in incest (I Corinthians 5). The second sin is unwillingness to reconcile with a brother or a sister (Matthew 18). If a person has sought reconciliation with another witness present, and finally before the combined authority of the body, the Scripture enjoins us to consider the one who will not be reconciled as a non-believer. We read, "Treat him as you would a pagan or a tax collector."

In Galatians we see that anyone who teaches a different gospel is to be anathema, or under a curse, and not considered part of the body. Thus anyone in gross doctrinal error, and not in accord with apostolic foundations in Scripture, is not to be accepted as a member of the body.

Scripture also gives the eldership judicial authority to decide disputes between members of the body. Believers are told not to take their disputes to civil courts, as this is a poor testimony. Paul said,

> "Therefore, if you have disputes about such matters, appoint as judges even men of little account in the church! I say this to shame you. Is it possible that there is nobody among you wise enough to judge a dispute between believers?" (I Corinthians 6:4,5)

Anyone who truly repents is to be received back into the body. However, for the sake of the glory of God and the power of the Spirit in the body, for healing those who want to walk in God's way, *the Scriptures give strong warning to not continue with those who claim to be believers but are immoral.* These are some Scriptures which demonstrate this:

> "But now I am writing you that you must not associate with anyone who calls himself a brother but is sexually immoral or greedy, an idolator or a slanderer, a drunkard or a swindler. With such a man do not even eat." (I Corinthians 5:10,11)

> "What business is it of mine to judge those outside the church? Are you not to judge those inside? God will judge those outside. Expel the wicked man from among you." (I Corinthians 5:11-13)

> "Warn a divisive person once, and then warn him a second time. After that, have nothing more to do with him. You may be sure that such a man is warped and sinful . . ."(Titus 3:10,11)

"I urge you brothers, to watch out for those who cause divisions and put obstacles in your way that are contrary to the teaching you have learned. Keep away from them. For such people are not serving our Lord Messiah, but their own appetites. By smooth talk and flattery they deceive the minds of naive people." (Romans 16:17,18)

"See to it that no bitter root grows up to cause trouble and defile many. See that no one is sexually immoral, or is godless . . ." (Hebrews 12:15,16)
(See also II John 10, II Peter 3:3 [scoffers], Jude 13, II Corinthians 13:11.)

A "bitter root" is manifest in causing factions, arguing, negative and destructive criticism, and weakness in succumbing to temptation. Such people cause disaster in congregations. Many congregations are weak because they do not allow biblical discipline to be applied in their midst and thus ruin God's testimony. The responsibility of discipline for such offenses is given to the elders. Members are enjoined to support their elders in the difficult and even painful tasks of discipline.

The key breakdown in body life is usually in the area of spreading unsubstantiated bad reports against other members and leaders. In receiving such reports others become poisoned and take up the case (reproach) against another. Scripture asks, "Lord, who may dwell in your sanctuary? The reply is, "He who . . . has no slander on his tongue, who does his neighbor no wrong and casts no slur on his fellow man . . ." (Psalm 15:1-3).

There are biblical means for addressing grievances against other members and leaders in the body. We will talk about this procedure shortly. Scripture is rigorous about avoiding gossip, slander, and receiving bad reports outside of proper biblical channels. Let's look at several passages which teach this:

Proverbs 26:17—"Like one who seizes a dog by the ears is a passer-by who meddles in a quarrel not his own."

Proverbs 18:13-17—"He who answers before listening—that is his folly and his shame . . . The heart of the discerning acquires knowledge . . . the first to present his case seems right, till another comes forward and questions him."

I Timothy 5:19—"Do not entertain an accusation against an elder unless it is brought by two or three witnesses.

Mark 4:24—"Consider carefully what you hear . . ."

Proverbs 22:10—"Drive out the mocker, and out goes strife; quarrels and insults are ended."

Proverbs 26:20—"Without wood a fire goes out; without gossip a quarrel dies down."

There is no place in the body for talking behind the backs of others unless it is among elders who are making a decision which affects the body. Scripture sets up clear channels for handling disputes, whether they are between members or in regard to leaders. We read in Matthew 18:15ff, the following procedure:

"If your brother sins against you, go and show him his fault, just between the two of you. If he listens to you, you have won your brother over. But if he will not listen, take one or two others along, so that every matter may be established by the testimony of two or three witnesses. If he refuses to listen to them, tell it to the church; and if he refuses to listen even to the church, treat him as you would a pagan or a tax collector."

Several things are apparent from this passage. First of all, disputes are to be kept on a level involving as few people as possible. Secondly, the phrase concerning *witness is in Jewish legal terms.* It has to do with leaders, as judges, hearing evidence. This means that testimony will ultimately be brought before the leadership to resolve the issue. As indicated in I Corinthians 6, the body's leadership is *to judge* the issue. Even accusations against elders are handled this way and the other elders can judge. Titus makes it clear we are not to spread dissension in the body but to use this channel. No accusation is to be received unless witnesses will testify and witnesses are only to be heard within the channels whereby a decision will be given.

Only by rigorously following such procedures in love is accusation used for purifying and correcting the body. Spreading accusations outside of the proper procedures only produces seeds of destruction in the body. This is why Paul told Timothy, "Do not entertain an accusation against an elder unless it is brought by two or three witnesses." (I Timothy 5:19).

Rebellion and sin are gutless. Rebellious persons do not try to obey these directions nor do they have the patience to handle things correctly. Roots of bitterness, perhaps from unforgiveness toward spouses or parents, spring up in bitterness toward all authority and poison the congregation. Yet Scripture enjoins us to "keep the unity of the Spirit through the bond of peace." (Ephesians 4:3).

When there is a disagreement with a leader or the leadership as a whole, the person should go to the leadership. He should have a prayerful attitude of love and humility in his approach. If the leadership as a whole is seriously in error scripturally, you may eventually have to leave the body. *Some leaders are willing to have elders from other congregations mediate serious disputes which involve them. This is helpful. However, if the disagreement is not a serious biblical error in doctrine or morality then the person has recourse to prayer.* Prayer is might and God will discipline, speak to, and even remove leaders from positions if they are in error or sin.

We should note that faith and flesh approach the question of authority very differently. Faith trusts God to use imperfect leaders as long as they are not in serious doctrinal error or immorality. The flesh, in pride, requires perfection of leaders and withholds submission until it is achieved. But we can always find imperfections in our leaders if we try to. Faith is willing to recognize those who show comparable spiritual superiority and who have developed abilities in group leadership or in coordination of other areas.

(The student should at this time read the qualifications for elders and shammashim in I Timothy 3:1-3.)

There are several safeguards to authority which we list here:

1. Authority is plural, so elders are mutually accountable to one another thus limiting abuse of authority.
2. The Scripture is the ultimate authority and members must leave a congregation in which elders violate Scripture.
3. Elder authority extends to the coordination of body life. The individual lives of members are not the province of elder authority unless members are in serious sin and error. Elders give individuals counsel, advice, and exhortation for their personal lives. But each individual must stand in conscience before God as recorded in Scripture. Authority which requires obedience in the personal details of one's life may be abusive.
4. There are channels of appeal when leaders are in serious moral or doctrinal error.
5. Prayer is powerful in improving situations.
6. God can remove elders who are or become unqualified. As long as serious sin is not being accepted by the leaders, one should be patient and wait, pray, and trust God to work problems out.

Peter said it well in I Peter 5:1-5:

"To the elders among you, I appeal as a fellow elder, a witness of Messiah's sufferings and one who also will share in the glory to be revealed: Be shepherds of God's flock that is under your care, serving as overseers—not because you must, but because you are willing, as God wants you to be; not greedy for money, but eager to serve; not lording it over those entrusted to you, but being examples to the flock. And when the Chief Shepherd appears, you will receive the crown of glory that will never fade away.

"Young men, in the same way be submissive to those who are older. Clothe yourselves with humility toward one another, because, 'God opposes the proud but gives grace to the humble.' "

May each elder be ready to serve the body in love, gentleness and firmness. May each member walk in love and forgiveness. The real key to unity in the body is to act in love and faith. No one who is loving slanders or causes division. He or she brings positive suggestion and criticism but never destruction. Those who walk in faith believe God will provide for the body. The answers to our questions concerning the nature of authority and submission, its extents and limits, are found in seeking to walk and speak according to the Bible.

A Word on the Role of the Head Pastor
In Ephesians four we read of the role of the pastor as one of the foundational gift ministries. The question of the pastor's role and authority in relationship to the rest of the leaders might be a question to many. We have seen excellent congregations function under three models, but believe the last one to be the best:

1. The head pastor is simply an elder who is freed for greater authority but has no greater authority than the other elders. They are co-equal.
2. The head elder is the final authority and decision-maker. Although he may receive counsel from other elders, his decision is final. He may or may not find accountability to other pastors in the area.
3. The pastor is the leader of the elders. It is his job to raise up and train the shepherds of the flock. This is reflected in Paul's instructions to Timothy and Titus in the letters addressed to them. However, although he is the leader of the elders, he cannot go forward without their affirma-

tion. There is a mutual accountability dimension between the pastor and the elders. Relationships of fellowship and accountability with other pastors are also of
great value. We never outgrow our need for accountability. Hence, our model is that the pastor's primary role is
to teach the flock in general and to equip the other leaders for ministry, but not to do the work of ministry on his
own.

STUDY QUESTIONS

1. The primary human authority in the body of believers is

   vested in _____

   _____

   _____

2. Give some Scriptural evidences that authority is invested in

   a plurality of elders. _____

   _____

   _____

   _____

3. What do we men when we say leadership in the body of

   believers is charismatic? _____

   _____

   _____

   _____

4. Name four functions of the eldership as we listed them.

   a. _____

b. _____

c. _____

d. _____

5. The Scriptures warn us not to associate with whom? _____

_____

_____

6. Spreading bad reports about others is forbidden in Scripture.

How are we to handle grievances properly? _____

_____

_____

_____

7. What is the difference between faith and flesh in our

approach to leaders? _____

_____

_____

8. Briefly summarize six safeguards against the abuse of
leadership.

a. _____

_____

_____

b. _____

_____

_____

c. _____

_____

_____

d. _____

_____

_____

e. _____

_____

_____

f. _____

_____

_____

VERSES FOR MEMORIZATION

I Corinthians 15:11
Romans 16:17,18
Hebrews 12:15
Psalm 15:1-3

SECTION C—COORDINATING BODY LIFE
HOW LEADERS ARISE—POSITIONS AND THE BODY
FOUR PITFALLS IN MESSIANIC JUDAISM

POSITIONS IN THE BODY

We know that Yeshua matured and learned obedience through what He suffered and thus was made perfect (Hebrews 5:8). In Yeshua, we see one who grew in submission to His parents, a learner and a listener before He became a teacher. Many people in the body of believers want positions of power or prominence. But until they learn maturity by servanthood toward the body, without prominence, they are dangerous choices for visible leadership roles. Yeshua said, "He that would be great among you, let him be a servant."

Leaders arise in the body as they demonstrate themselves to be consistent servants in love. Those who will not pull together in unity as non-prominent parts of the body have no business desiring prominence! Some people are catapulted into leadership roles having no history of significant involvement in body life. Only when a person has proven himself a consistent and humble servant, does God call such a person to a leadership role. Leadership roles are given as a person demonstrates in measure that he or she has the necessary gifts by functioning in capacities which lead to future leadership positions.

For example, an elder may arise as follows: A person comes to know the Lord. *He demonstrates responsible stewardship in the body. Perhaps he serves as a member of a committee, or on an outreach team. He may as well show special hospitality by opening up his home to show healing love to others.* Others begin to speak well of such a person and the eldership as a whole begins to *recognize the gifts* and spiritual maturity of the person. If his home life is in order, perhaps he will be called upon to give himself to lead a committee, coordinate a specific congregational area, or serve as shammash.

An ordered home life is crucial because order or disorder in this area produce order and disorder in the body. If the person serves well in the responsibility he is given, if others gravitate to him for counsel and healing love, and if he is able to convey the truths of the Word, the elders may appoint him as an elder, with congregational affirmation if their body includes this. A similar process may occur for shammashim and the appointment of other leaders such as music leaders, committee chairpersons, and other coordinators.

There are times when a person functioning in a leadership capacity is seen as not functioning adequately. Perhaps his home life is in disarray. Or it could be he has become proud and attached in the flesh to his position. In such a case, instead of the fruits of the Spirit being produced by his ministry, the manifestations of the flesh become apparent. When such is the case, it is usually the elders who perceive the problem first, although a segment of the congregation may perceive it as well. The moral sin may be critical, but not gross, which would require either public repentance or exclusion from the body (I Corinthians 5:11ff).

For the sake of the health of the body and the individual, it is crucial that the elders be able to remove such a person from his leadership position. This situation is one which continually occurs in many congregations. It should not cause problems, however, carnality and sin often lead to rebellion in what is an obvious matter of elder authority.

How does the problem of a person functioning inadequately in a leadership capacity manifest itself?

1. The person proves the elders right by being unwilling to accept their recommendations. He really is in pride attached to his position. Behind the elders' backs, he gives a one-sided, unfair account of his removal and the reasons for it. He is able to find others who are not obedient to the Scriptures to take up an offense for him. The carnal find each other, they gravitate to each other and form a faction encouraging one another in their carnality. This puts the elders in a tremendous bind. Do they divulge the private reasons for their decision, to allay the half-truths being spread? This would be biblical, but often the desire to be "merciful" causes the leaders to be reluctant to divulge the facts.
2. Perhaps the elders acted rightly but should have acted

sooner. Repenting of their lack of courage earlier solves this problem.

3. Perhaps the congregants do not accept the decision because they hold to a democratic model and feel they should vote on even matters which have private dimensions involved with them. It is crucial congregants do not receive bad reports and that the elders be given latitude in their decisions in these regards. If the elders are wrong, the person removed can prove them so by:

   a. Accepting the decision as within the providence and discipline of God.
   b. Growing in faith by seeking God's comfort.
   c. Continuing to humbly serve the body.

By responding this way the person and the body will grow; perhaps he will be restored to leadership with new power and anointing from God. In no way should baby believers be given the right to debate personal issues or issues involving positions of leadership when such issues have private counseling dimensions.

Unity, peace, and love in the body are paramount. And as we have said, there are biblical procedures for redressing grievances. Spreading and accepting half-truths and forming factions are never the solution. The glory of God is at stake! (See Hebrews 13:17, I Corinthians 3:3 on factions.)

God is capable, through our faith and prayers, of redressing wrongs. Elders may be removed over the years by non-affirmation or by other means. We must have faith to believe God will work through the authority structure as seen in Scripture. We must pull in unity behind those God has ordained. And we must never become committed to narrow positions, only to the service of the Lord.

FOUR PROBLEM TYPES IN MESSIANIC JUDAISM

Every congregation deals with common problems. The Scripture says no test has overtaken us but that which is common to man (I Corinthians 10:13). This statement can be applied to congregations as well as to individuals. However, in Messianic congregations there are unique manifestations of common problems. In our experience, we have found controversy and tensions arising primarily from four groups of people. They are the anti-charismatic legalists, the super-charismatic rebellious, and the anti-Jewish Jews, and the super-Jewish Jews. These groups greatly unsettle the members of the body unless the members are clear about their positions.

The first two types are common problems in all congregations. By describing these types you will be able to avoid becoming one of them, be able to give help to them, and not be as easily unsettled from your own position.

Of course, the reader should understand that the descriptions that follow are generalizations. Yet there is significant insight, though not by any measure exhaustive understanding, through these generalizations.

The anti-charismatic legalist is a person who is rigid. Any manifestation of the Spirit upsets such a person and the mistakes which sometimes occur from allowing periods of freedom in a worship service can turn him into raging anger. This person questions manifestations of the Spirit in a skeptical, and perhaps cynical spirit. In addition, this person often majors in the minors by becoming embroiled in arguments over fine points of theological interpretation. Indeed, this person relishes a knowledge of mostly detailed, "intellectualist" significance. The source of this mentality is the lack of *real love faith relationship with God.* The intellect, a valid part of our God-given abilities, has become dominant over the spirit and the emotions. Such a believer may appear cold and rigid, but his suppressed feelings manifest themselves in anger at others.

Several causes form such an imbalance: the lack of warm, loving parents, an over-emphasis on the intellectual in upbringing, an engrained pride in detailed knowledge, a fear of embarrassment, and a fear of the unpredictable. This person's pride is greatly *offended* when anything is not done in an appropriate way. The solution for this person is counsel from an understanding and honest person. He can break out of this problem by cultivating a real love for and trust in God.

The super-charismatic rebellious is an emotionally dominated type. The exact opposite of the anti-charismatic legalist, this person demonstrates an impatience with all form. Quiet reflective worship is rejected as being dead. This person always believes himself to be hearing from God, yet his life is characterized by great instability. Rarely will he settle down in one congregation, but if he does, he wants to dominate it.

This person is constantly given over to emotional prophecy, prayer, and words from the Lord. Any attempt to correct error on his part is met with the reply that the elders are "quenching the Spirit." But the elders are told to "test the spirits" (I Timothy 4:1), and the spirits of the prophets are subject to the prophets. Usually such a person is manifest by refusing to come under the authority or discipline of any congregation. Underlying his behavior is often a lack of discipline and attention in home life. He is rebellious, craves attention, and seeks a sense of self-worth through delusions of self-importance. This person gives fuel to the anti-charismatic legalist who uses him as an example in arguing for a preclusion of charismatic freedom.

The anti-Jewish Jew is a person who finds Jewish practices to be worthless. The question can be asked, "What is such a person doing in a Messianic congregation?" The answer is, his self-rejection does not allow him to accept his own identity and heritage, but neither does it allow him to totally assimilate out of fear the Gentile community would not accept him. In its most severe form, such a person from a harsh, unloving upbringing, literally gets sick during Jewish hymns and other celebrations. But he rationalizes his problem as a "perception in the Spirit" that the congregation is engaging in dead, worthless things. He may even have anti-Semitic opinions of Jewish people and a great deal of self-hate.

In milder forms, perhaps this person was rapped on the knuckles by a stern Hebrew teacher or made to sit through hours of services in a language he could not understand. Jewish prayer, forms, and holidays only bring back bad memories of emptiness. This person often projects this emptiness into the body as a whole and puts a spiritual construction on the situation saying these Jewish things are dead. These things may be rich to others, but not to him. His model of a Messianic congregation is a more neutral congregation without crosses and pictures of Jesus, and also without Jewish traditions of value.

Sometimes this person finds himself in league with the super-charismatic because of their rejection of all form. There may be rebellion toward parents and heritage in the severe case, or just disinterest toward Jewish things in a milder case. If such a person cannot come to understand the sources of his reaction or disinterest and overcome it (a worthwhile goal), he would do better to grow in a non-Jewish context of body life.

The super-Jewish Jew is totally caught up in the fact that he is a Jew. There is a great pride in being a Jew to such an extent that real spiritual issues and dimensions are absent or overlooked. Such a person unthinkingly gravitates to support anything that has been or is Jewish. In some cases he is anti-Gentile and fights the world with Jewish self-assertion. Rather than gaining a primary identity in a deep love and trust relationship with the Lord, he has misunderstood involvement in Jewish forms as spirituality itself.

This person does not root his Jewish identity primarily in the biblical dimensions of the call to be Jewish (which will be explained in chapter seven), but rather in fostering orthopraxy. He may try to push the congregation into an orthodox worship form despite the objections of the congregants. He may adopt a rigid Rabbinic style.

But there is often a great deal of inconsistency in this person's life, even hypocrisy. For example, although he pushes orthopraxy, he will work on the Sabbath. There is a lack of a real faith dimension to his living, life is lived by self-striving after the flesh. This may issue in a new legalism. Often the super Jew is found in intense confrontation with anti-Jews and super-charismatics. But he finds an ally in the legalistic anti-charismatic, even though he may intellectually claim to accept the charismatic dimension.

This person fears constantly that the Messianic congregation will lose its Jewishness. If a Jewish hymn or form is skipped one week or if a chorus is sung which is not specifically Jewish, he feels *great* consternation. What is the underlying problem? In all probability, this person is still conforming out of fear to domineering parents whose messages are still embedded in his mind. The fear of reprisals from Dad, Mom, or the Rabbi, still determine his thinking. So often, we hear complaints concerning the congregation about what a Jewish religious person will think if they see us clap hands, or sing this or leave out that. Usually they think nothing of it.

The real issue is, "What would Dad or Mom think if they saw me participating in something so *visibly* lacking in ortho-praxy?" Yet the Sabbath can be broken (because it is a private act), but do not change visible public forms! The super-Jewish Jew lacks a real faith-love relationship with God. He has undervalued the important and overvalued and reacts to the minor. Often he is an unstable person in the other dimensions of his life, such as marriage and work.

This person needs counsel and love to overcome this prob-lem. There must be a commitment to know the Messiah, and to count all else as worthless in comparison (Philippians 3:8). He must repent of works-righteousness and pride as well.

When a congregation has a predominance of these four types, it can literally be destroyed. It is important that the leadership set a clear and balanced direction and not be diverted by those whose viewpoint is a product of imbalance and emotional scars. Our advice to you as the student is to seek those highest values first: the love of God, service to others in love and the spreading of the Good News. Do not be diverted by individuals with these problems. And if you find tendencies toward any of these types of problems in yourself, seek the help of a knowledgeable and empathetic counselor.

STUDY QUESTIONS

1. How do leaders arise in the body? _____

   _____

   _____

2. Why is it necessary that elders have the latitude to remove

   people from positions of leadership in the body? _____

   _____

   _____

3. What are three improper responses to elder decisions with
   regard to leaders being removed from positions?

   a. _____

   _____

   b. _____

   _____

   c. _____

   _____

4. What is the proper response on the part of a person who is

   removed from a position? _____

   _____

   _____

   _____

5. Name the four major problem types in Messianic Judaism and give a sentence definition of each.

a. _____

   _____

   _____

b. _____

   _____

   _____

c. _____

   _____

   _____

   _____

d. _____

   _____

   _____

   _____

   _____

TO LIVE AS A JEW

1. LIVING AS A JEW

The Messianic Jew has a glorious call of God to reenact the history of God's revelation. He, of all Jews, should not seek to insecurely assert a vague or unbased identity. He knows he is a member of a sign people who demonstrate God's faithfulness. His involvements in the community of Israel should be motivated by a love for God and for his own people. His celebrations through the calendar year are done in a way to extol fulfillment in Yeshua. *They are celebrations of God's grace in history for Israel and for all peoples.* This is his history, and this is God's history. *Re-enactment* is a key term in understanding the nature of Jewish celebration; *re-enactment in gratitude.* At Passover, we remember we died and rose with Yeshua and that *we* came out of Egypt in our ancestors. The same God continues to deliver us today.

The Messianic Jew must not be put on the defensive by foolish statements by brothers and sisters who lack understanding. Here are few examples:

> "You are to extol Jesus, any emphasis which takes away from just praising Jesus is a diversion."
> "Your identity is in Jesus. All other identities are false."

These statements are blatantly wrong. Yes, we are to love Yeshua. However, who is the Yeshua we love? Is He an abstract being? Are we loving the "Jesus" and not the real person? Jesus was and is, Yeshua the *Jew*. He is the one who wore fringes, healed on the Sabbath, and celebrated the Passover. God Himself is forever the God of Abraham, Isaac, and Jacob (cf. Exodus

3:10-14). We extol God for His *whole* involvement with humanity, from creation, the Exodus, and especially in the death and
resurrection of Yeshua.

We do not collapse the whole Bible into the word "Jesus."
Sometimes we get the feeling some people are in love with the
word "Jesus" and the feelings this word elicits, without loving
the person in all the facets revealed in Scripture. The full
identity of Jesus and of God leads us to memorialize *all* of the
Bible's history.

Of course our identity is now in Yeshua primarily. This
supersedes all other points of identity and makes them pale in
comparison. It puts us into a unity with all other believers
which must be maintained in relationships and acts of love. But
we do injustice to the uniqueness of every individual if we
dissolve all other aspects of his uniqueness. A true appreciation
of a person respects every part of personality which is good. I
am a follower of Yeshua. I am a Jew. I am an American. I am a
man. I am a teacher. I am a Redskins' football fan. I am an avid
camper. I am a tennis enthusiast. I am a student of economics.
To deny a personality in all its facets is to reject the person and
all of the richness of variety God has created.

*Such denial arises from an insecurity which must have
everyone else be like us.* It desires a boring, totalitarian same-
ness in all persons. But in our humanity we are male and
female, Jew and non-Jew, black and white, sports enthusiasts
and art enthusiasts. Humanity is a *symphonic* reality, not an
orchestra made up of all violins. Of all human identities, being a
Jew is certainly the least to be forsaken. This is because God is
the God of Israel, Yeshua is representative Israel, and all who
accept Him become part of commonwealth Israel and are connected to the historic nation.

This introduction to the following section leads us to consider the nature of the covenants. If one is under a new covenant, doesn't this do away with the old?

THE BIBLICAL COVENANTS

First of all, there is more than one old covenant. There are
many old covenants, many of which are still in effect. All of the
covenants stem from God's mercy and grace and they ask for

obedience in response. Let's look at this pattern in several covenants:

In Genesis 9 we read about the *Noahic Covenant.* God offered a gracious agreement in which He promised never again to destroy the world by flood. The people were to avoid the eating of blood (reverence for life) and not permit a murderer to live.

In Genesis 12, 15, and 17, we read of the *Abrahamic Covenant.* In this covenant Abraham was promised the land of Israel in his descendants, a nation to come from his seed which would be preserved forever. Also he would be a blessing through his descendants to all people (especially in Yeshua) and God would bless others in relation to their response to Israel. The response to this covenant was to be obedient to God and circumcision. Circumcision was the outward sign of the covenant. This is an everlasting covenant still in effect today.

The *Mosaic Covenant* materials are found in Exodus through Deuteronomy. These materials are founded on the act of God's grace in the Exodus and Passover, events which established and freed the nation of Israel. Undergoing these experiences together molded Israel into national unity. The memory of what God had done was Israel's basis for existence. Israel's response to God's grace was to be national and personal obedience to the injunctions of God in the Torah. *This included universal moral and social commands which are a reflection of God's standard and character by which all human beings are judged.*

These standards are still reflected in the life of those who are obedient in Yeshua. The Torah also includes Israel's national celebrations of God's grace in this history. In addition, it included provisions for the temple sacrifice which pointed to Yeshua. The Mosaic covenantal order was replaced by a New Covenantal order after Yeshua became our sacrifice and priest (Hebrews 9). However, the new order assumes the validity of the continued existence of Israel and its celebration of God's work in history. It catches up as part of itself those aspects of the Mosaic order which have continuing validity.

In II Samuel 7, David was promised an everlasting throne. This covenant is fulfilled in Yeshua, the son of David, and is commonly called the *Davidic Covenant*. Let's look at the New Covenant more closely.

THE PROMISE OF A NEW COVENANT

The need for a new covenant was anticipated by the Torah itself. Before Israel had even entered the Promised Land, Moses foresaw its national faithlessness toward God's covenant. Thus, the book of Deuteronomy called for a circumcision of the heart (Deuteronomy 30:4-6) in which the calloused flesh of the heart was cut away and an attitude of pliable love and obedience toward God would arise.

But as Israel's history progressed, their continued failure readied the prophets to receive revelation of something more to come. Israel was depleted by idolatry. First the nation was split into north and south, and then came the captivity of the northern tribes and an end to their national existence. Finally, in 586 B.C.E., the national life of the southern kingdom ended when the king of Babylon conquered the last vestiges of the nation.

The prophets of God spoke in the context of these tragic events. Joel foresaw an age in which the power of the Spirit of God would be more universally given to all (Joel 2:28,29). Most striking, however, are the parallel promises in Jeremiah and Ezekiel of the New Covenant to be offered to Israel. Jeremiah ministered to the last remnant in the land of Israel before their final demise in 586 B.C.E. Ezekiel ministered at the same time in Babylonia to those taken captive. Despite the seeming hopelessness due to Israel's national demise and the failure of Israel in its call from God, both prophets predicted a resurrection of Israel's national life. The dry bones vision in Ezekiel 37 and the prediction of the limit of 70 years of captivity by Jeremiah offered hope. Israel would live (Am Yisrael chai).

Both predicted a new covenant, B'rit Chadashah. It is true that Messianic Jews believe that the B'rit Chadashah has been established by the life, death and resurrection of Yeshua. However, it is also true that not all the features of the new covenant have been fully established. In regard to the presence of the kingdom, only a partial but central part of this covenant has been fulfilled. That all Israelites shall personally know God through it, it is not yet fulfilled.

It is not our purpose in this section to fully outline the relationship of old covenants to the New Covenant. We only want to lay out the structure of the New Covenant in its original context as background material for future exposition. Any interpretation of the New Covenant which contradicts the clear meaning of Jeremiah 31 and Ezekiel 36 must be amiss. Our outline comes from these passages.

First, the New Covenant is with the house of Israel and Judah (Jeremiah 31:31). It may be offered as well to other nations as a way into fellowship with God, but this certainly is not the emphasis of these passages. The Messianic Age does include Gentiles who have fellowship with God in the age of Israel's full restoration, but an age for the exclusive offer of salvation to Gentiles is not presented there.

Second, the covenant is *different* from the *Mosaic* covenant which God made after Exodus.

Third, this difference is God's law or Torah being written on the hearts of the people of the nation (Jeremiah 33:33). Ezekiel said, "I will give you a new heart and put a new spirit in you; I will remove from you your heart of stone and give you a heart of flesh. . . ." He continued with the promise that God would move them to follow "My decrees and be careful to keep My laws." The New Covenant is therefore not an abrogation of Torah but an ability to walk in Torah! What a contrast to common teachings today. However, does it mean Torah in the general sense of God's ways (reflected in the books of Moses), or is it the whole Mosaic system? Before Moses, Abraham, in Genesis 26:5, was told to obey God's Charge, commandments, statutes and laws. The rabbis debated whether or not Torah would be altered in the Messianic Age. Some thought parts of the Torah had a temporary relevance to an imperfect people, but in the Messianic Age, we would be so close to God, that Torah would be altered to fit this situation. Basically those aspects of Mosaic teaching that have continuing validity are assumed as part of the new covenant (Ezekiel 36). It suffices at this point to emphasize *the New Covenant is Torah-positive, not Torah-negative.*

Ezekiel added a fourth promise: that we would have a new spirit, which is parallel to being given a new heart. And fifth,

God would put his Spirit within us.

Sixth, the New Covenant includes the promise to Israel to dwell in their own land in safety and security (v.24-28). *Thus God's Name is to be vindicated among the nations* through His work in Israel as a nation. What a contrast for those who hold that the New Covenant does away with national Israel!

Seventh, the reception of the New Covenant brings forgiveness of sin and cleansing from iniquity (Jeremiah 31:34, Ezekiel 36:25), whereby Israel will be God's people and God will be Israel's Lord.

In contrasting this covenant to the Mosaic the prophets clearly had in mind the extent to which this covenant *would fulfill God's purposes for Israel.* Was forgiveness offered under the Mosaic system? Yes. Was there an ability to love and do God's law? Yes, if we are to believe David's meditation in Psalm 19 and 119. Yet even David grievously sinned.

The New Covenant would come with a *power* of forgiveness never known before. The Spirit would be given in a direct and powerful way to all, as never before. This would enable a direct intuitive knowledge of God in changed hearts to an *extent* and at a *level* never known before. This covenant would be fully effective in producing the life which the Mosaic covenant did not produce. How utterly exciting is the hope of the prophets! This New Covenant is offered in Yeshua ha Mashiach! The New Testament shows clearly that it includes Jew and Gentile.

WHO IS A JEW?

Much confusion is caused by the questions, who is a Jew and what does it mean to live as a Jew.

According to Halachah (traditional Jewish legal interpretation), a person is Jewish if born of a Jewish mother, circumcised if a male, and not a convert to another religion. Some Rabbinic authorities have been willing to consider the convert to another religion as still Jewish, but would definitely not consider his children Jewish. This definition is also expanded to include those who convert to Judaism through instruction, decision, the ritual Mikvah (Jewish water immersion), and circumcision. But there are problems with this position.

The major problem is contradiction to the Scriptural indications that Jewish descent was carried through the father. The covenant was originally made with Abraham. The father clearly determined the religious identity of his family. The covenant sign of circumcision was applied to the male member indicating this was a covenant applying to physical descendants through the father.

Many Israelites of prominence took non-Jewish wives who then were part of the Jewish identity of the family with no formal conversion. This is so with the wife of Moses who was a Cushite. It is also true of Ruth with Boaz, the ancestors of David the king. That Jewish identity can be passed on through the father is especially clear in the case of Athaliah, the wicked pagan queen descended from Jezebel. Through her came Ahaziah the king and an ancestor of the Messiah. Though Athaliah sought to destroy the royal Messianic line, her grandson Joash survived and became king. Certainly no one can claim Jezebel and Athaliah were legitimate converts to Judaism, yet Athaliah's son and grandson were Jews! Therefore we must add to the traditional definition of who is a Jew, the element of descent from the father.

It is true, though, that the definition of who is a Jew must include more than just physical descent and circumcision if we are to carry on the identity of Jewishness. For even nations and tribes have converted to Judaism and were then considered part of Israel. Through the years by marriage, the children of these converts also became partakers of the blood line from Abraham. What is important to note is that others would become part of the nation of Israel.

David Ben Gurion, when asked who is a Jew, was so loose in his definition he simply stated a Jew was anyone who desired to identify himself as a Jew. This seems to overlook the seriousness of taking of Jewish identity with real conviction.

Why then did the Halachic definition define Jewish descent through the mother alone? The reason reaches back to Ezra. At that time the Jewish remnant which returned to the land was being influenced toward an adulteration of their religious purity through the influence of spouses. Ezra commanded the men to divorce and send away their non-Jewish wives. The conclusion of Rabbis was that their children would then not be considered Jewish. It was also thought the mother's early upbringing of the child, as well as the certainty of the child's descent from the mother, but uncertainty in the case of the father's identity, all lent weight toward adopting this viewpoint. Suffice it to say the Scriptural role of the father and descent from the father is also crucial.

WHAT DOES IT MEAN TO BE JEWISH?

The question of who is a Jew is not more important than what it means to be Jewish or to live as a Jew. In seeking to answer this question we are not, as sometimes accused, saying that someone who does not live a Jewish life is not Jewish, any more than an American who is not patriotic is not an American. We do feel that a person who does not live as a Jew weakens the sense of Jewish identity among his family and undercuts the perpetuation of a unique and identifiable Jewish people. We must all do our part in being faithful to our calling, passing down the Jewish heritage, and strengthening the community.

There are many answers given as to what it means to be a Jew. Some see support of Israel and Jewish community causes as central, others point to synagogue attendance or celebration of the feasts. All of these responses are partially true, but the full truth is only seen in light of Scripture's teaching. The fullest sense of what it means to be a Jew is biblically defined.

As stated many times throughout these chapters, God has called Israel to be a unique nation among the nations; a witness to His truth and faithfulness. Furthermore, as a nation she was given unique practices, such as the practice of the Sabbath and the feasts, so that they would be unified by the memory of what God had done in graciously establishing them as a nation. She would also then be unified in recognizing her unique purpose in showing forth the truth of the Scriptures and the faithfulness of God. The biblical heritage of feast and festival and identity with the nation is crucial.

If we ask what makes up a nation from a sociological point of view, we gain further insight. In light of the fact God has committed Himself to preserve the nation of Israel, and that we desire to be in accord with this purpose, these insights are important. A nation in its strongest sense usually requires three major elements: defined borders, a common language, and a common culture and heritage. Weakening any of these strands which constitute a nation weakens the survival of the nation.

Currently, for example, we can see the weakness of Canada due to the cultural and linguistic differences between French and English-speaking Canadians. Historically, nations have disappeared when uprooted from their land. Israel is unique because she maintained her nationhood though uprooted. The Jews were not in Israel, but the land of Israel was within the Jews! Hence, the importance of national borders was less crucial in Israel's case because the land of Israel became part of Israel's religious-cultural hope.

Israel in the diaspora was preserved by God. How? Through a common language and a common heritage. Although Hebrew was not Israel's spoken language, it was maintained as the language of the synagogue. A Jew could worship in Russia, Poland, France or England with no language barrier. In addition, the biblical practices of feasting and fasting as well as the Rabbinic tradition, some of which we might take issue with, provided for amazing cultural continuity. This was the case even when the fullness of the biblical meaning of Israel's call as a nation was lost. This common heritage gave rise to a universal sense of Jewish brotherhood which continues to this day in Jewish community concerns for those in need, support for Israel within her ancient borders, and the maintaining of other Jewish cultural ties in music, dance, and literature.

The full scope of being a loyal Jew includes involvement in the Jewish community and support for Israel. However, it means *as well* the preservation of the very historic-biblical roots of our heritage which make these involvements possible. It also includes Sabbath, the feasts, Hebrew weddings, bar mitzvah's, unique tunes and sounds in worship, as well as Bible-based discerning appreciation of Jewish history, literature, and wisdom. Not all will be able to fully give themselves to the whole of the Jewish heritage, but as loyal Jews, we do so to the extent that we can in the Spirit's leading.

God has preserved Israel, but He has done so through the

elements of Jewish heritage. Being a Jew is not just a physical thing. Messianic Jews must be on guard against tailoring their identity to a meaning weak in heritage, because of the influence of Jews who become believers and are weak in their identifying with Jewish heritage. This weakness has to be countered if there is to be a viable Messianic Judaism. No amount of ignorant comment concerning the "dead nature of Jewish tradition," "coming under bondage of the law," and other such misapplications of Scripture, should shake us from recognizing the biblical and spiritual calling we have from God to love and be part of the heritage of our people. Israel's calendar is from God. Her preservation through her heritage is also from God. She is therefore a unique witness to God's faithfulness and His Lordship over all of history. "For God's gifts and His call (to Israel) are irrevocable." (Romans 11:29).

Also central to the Jewish heritage is the prophetic call to social righteousness, concern for justice, compassion, and mercy. Biblical law is a foundation of social law for many western nations. Messianic Jews should be in the forefront of witnessing to these prophetic truths.

However, as Messianic Jews we can creatively appropriate our heritage as we are led by the Spirit. It must come from within, rather than artificially and rotely imposed from without. We must not feel in bondage to do things as other groups do them.

STUDY QUESTIONS

1. Jewish celebration is primarily re _____
   of God's history. Explain this further.

   _____

   _____

2. Name four covenants in the Tenach (Old Testament).

   a. _____

   b. _____

   c. _____

   d. _____
3. Name several aspects of the Mosaic covenant.

   a. _____

   b. _____

   c. _____

   d. _____
4. Name seven aspects of the New Covenant.

   a. _____

   b. _____

   c. _____

   d. _____

   e. _____

   f. _____

    g. _____

5. How is the New Covenant contrasted with the Mosaic? ____

_____

_____

6. List several features of what it means to live as a Jew.

    a. _____

    b. _____

    c. _____

    d. _____

    e. _____

    f. _____

VERSES FOR MEMORIZATION

Acts 28:17
Read and meditate on Acts 21:17-26

SECTION B—JEWISH FEASTS AND PRACTICES

Historically Israel's year was punctuated by marvelous annual celebrations. All of them were occasions of great thanksgiving as well as times for additional sacrifices related to atonement, forgiveness, and dedication.

Leviticus 23 gives an outline of these special times. *Sabbath*, though a weekly feast, was considered the most prominent Holy day other than Yom Kippur. *Pesach*, or Passover, and the feast of unleavened bread were also prominent.

Passover was the great annual commemoration of the events connected to Israel's Exodus from Egypt. The feast recalls the angel of death passing over the homes of the Israelites who had the Passover lamb's blood upon their doors. The meal of bitter herbs commemorated the bitter life of slavery from which Israel was freed. The lamb was a parallel meal to the Exodus meal and the unleavened bread paralleled the unleavened bread eaten when Israel left Egypt. The Israelites left in such haste that their bread had no time to rise. This was Israel's independence day. Since the Exodus was God's means of establishing the nation, Passover, as well as the other Holy days, was to be celebrated "forever and to all your generations (l'olam v'ed) by the nation."

It is possible that "forever" had reference to a people under the Mosaic sacrificial system and once it was replaced, the "forevers" were of no further legal importance, since the Mosaic system was no longer in force. After all, the sacrifices under the Aaronic priesthood are also commanded to be carried on forever. How shall we evaluate the "forever" commands?

Although the "forevers" are to be taken seriously, they do not constitute final proof. There is another dimension in understanding the feasts which is especially apparent in regard to Passover. *Although the feasts are part of the Mosaic system they are also indissolubly bound up with the Abrahamic covenant.* The Abrahamic covenant promised a nation to Abraham and the Exodus was predicted as a means of fulfilling the promise. Passover is the celebration of the fulfillment of the promise to Abraham! If we take the Abrahamic covenant seriously, holding that Israel is promised the land and still chosen of God as a nation, it is inconsistent to do away with celebrations of the fulfillment of God's promises to Abraham.

Every nation has its days of special celebration which are part of its national distinctiveness. But numerous are the Christians who twist the Abrahamic covenant which is unconditional, through either spiritualizing Scripture or ignoring it. Many more believe the Abrahamic covenant is still in effect and yet believe the celebrations of the faithfulness of God to that covenant are not valid. The other feasts are celebrations of Israel's national life under God in fulfillment of God's promise to Abraham. They are a unique part of Israel's calling and identity as a nation called of God.

An assembling of the people usually begins and ends most feasts. The Feast of Firstfruits, directly following Passover, included an offering of the first products of the earth to God. Through it the whole of the produce of Israel was acknowledged as God's and as His gift to the people.

Shavouth was the feast of the first harvest. It was a thanksgiving feast which came 50 days after Passover. It later was associated with the time of God's giving of the Torah. It is no accident that God also gave His Spirit to Yeshua's first followers on this same day, beginning a spiritual harvest through the Holy Spirit who would enable the Torah to be written upon our hearts. It is thus a feast of the Spirit as well.

Sukkoth was the third major feast. Its significance was agricultural as well as historical. This feast celebrated in thanksgiving the final harvest of the year. Israel was to dwell in tents or booths during a seven-day period. A great assembly followed. This practice recalled the wilderness wanderings of the nation. At that time Israel had no material possessions; trust in God was the only recourse. Wonderfully Israel was supernaturally given food (manna) as well as the miracle that their clothing did not wear out. God instituted this feast so Israel might remember that "adonai yirah," God is provider. In their own homes and lands, Israel's citizens were to always remember their existence depended upon God's grace, not upon their own wealth or self-efforts. Sukkoth was also a time of great sacrifices of thanksgiving, a truly joyous and festive occasion.

Israel's feasts are *all of grace*: God's grace in the Exodus miracle, God's grace in the harvest provisions, and God's grace in providing for all our needs. The feasts were the greatest celebrations of God's grace the world had ever seen. But no legalism about them was intended. The feasts were also great didactic lessons for each generation so Israel's history was given reality for each generation! Let's take a more detailed look at each of them.

SHABBAT:

The Sabbath is a central pivot of Jewish life. As taught by Yeshua, "the Sabbath was made for man and not man for the Sabbath." (Matthew 12). It was never meant to be a day of legalistic conformity. However, Sabbath is a day of crucial significance to Jewish identity. The principle of *weekly rest, worship and renewal has universal significance*. In this sense the Sabbath principle is a *spiritual and humanitarian guide for all peoples*. Christians are free to incorporate this principle on Sunday or other days.

The seventh day Sabbath for Israel is a special *sign of the covenant* between Israel and God. Thus to abrogate the sign of the covenant is to cast doubt on whether or not we uphold the continuing covenant of God with Israel. Sabbath itself antedates Israel's existence and is a reflection of the creation order. However, Israel is also given Sabbath as a memorial of God's gracious rescue from slavery, as well as a memorial of creation and God's resting in the seventh period.

Messianic Judaism looks to Yeshua, who proclaimed Himself "Lord of the Sabbath" (Mark 2), for direction in observance of Sabbath. The day is meant to be a break from the routine of work whereby we may be renewed through worship, fellowship and rest. By this rest and renewal, Messianic Jews testify that *God is Lord of creation and man need not be subject to work as though the economic sphere of life has tyrannical control over his life.* The person of faith knows the "rest of faith" in Yeshua testifies to the world that God is gracious and kind and provides for us by faith, even if he spends 1/7 of his life in freedom from providing for his own material needs.

In Exodus 20:8-11, the nature of Sabbath is described as *a testimony to God's Lordship over creation.* Hence all believers testify against theories of atheism, agnosticism, evolutionary naturalism, and pantheism, by upholding the truth that "In the beginning God created the heavens and the earth." (Genesis 1:1).

In Exodus 5:12-15, the Sabbath as *a memorial of the Exodus*, as well as a *humanitarian stipulation*, is stressed. On this day, rich and poor, freeman and slave, achieve a measure of equality in freedom from the domination of work. Sabbath is an essential faith principle. We believe God's word sufficiently to let go of our anxiety for food, clothes, and shelter, believing He is our loving Father and provider and we need not fear!

In the prophets we find the basic importance of Sabbath reaffirmed. Isaiah said, "Blessed is . . . the man . . . who keeps the Sabbath without desecrating it, and keeps his hand from doing any evil." He went on to delineate the blessings which shall be received by those who love God's covenant and express it in a heartfelt recognition of Sabbath.

We also read in Isaiah 58:13:

> "If you keep your feet from breaking the Sabbath and from doing as you please on My holy day, if you call the Sabbath a delight and the Lord's holy day honorable, and if you honor it by not going your own way and not doing as you please or speaking idle words, then you will find your joy in the Lord, and I will cause you to ride on the heights of the land and to feast on the inheritance of your father Jacob. The mouth of the Lord has spoken."

The prophets knew the desecration of the Sabbath struck at the heart of Israel's faith as to whether or not God was Lord, and whether or not Israel was God's covenant people!

The pages of the New Testament do not contradict the sense of Sabbath given in the Tenach. Yeshua criticized the legalists who made Sabbath a burden instead of a delight by multiplying legalistic restrictions. The Pharisees criticized His disciples for eating grain as they walked through the fields. Their actions were a natural response unconnected with work, *but the legalism of the day constituted this harvesting. Yeshua knew such legalism caused people to be concerned with restrictions, thereby missing the true meaning of the day: joy, refreshment, and renewal. As Lord of the Sabbath, Yeshua set the record straight.* The Sabbath is appropriate in a Messianic Jewish context for keeping alive these meanings.

Outside of a Jewish context, the Apostle Paul allowed for freedom in regard to worship days. Nowhere does he speak against Jews who follow the Sabbath. He did not, however, allow a legalistic imposition of Sabbath on non-Jews. Our historical documents show that the Jewish believers of the first several centuries continued to practice Sabbath as part of their heritage and witness.

In non-Jewish communities the Jewish influence was such that the seven-day week became universal. Even the Sabbath principle was adopted by the Church although its day of worship is Sunday. What is important is that Sunday in Christian practice is also one day in seven for worship, renewal and rest.

How is it that Christendom adopted the first day of the week as its day of worship? Some believe the early believers gathered on Sunday morning to celebrate the resurrection and celebrated both on the Sabbath and on Sunday. However, it is said the church believed that under the New Covenant the seventh day Sabbath had been abrogated and Sunday was a proper replacement of it.

Most recent scholarship suggests this explanation is mistaken. Dr. Samuel Bacchiocchi has written a definitve work on all of the evidence involved. A summary of his work appeared in the *Biblical Archaeology Review* (September/October 1978), and a fascinating debate ensued in the following issues.

The basic evidence seems to be that Sunday worship was not introduced as an authoritative apostolic practice. Part of the evidence is that "Paul refused to take a stand on the question of observance of days, advising rather to follow one's convictions and to respect differences of viewpoint." (Romans 14:3,5,6,10-13,19-21, 2:16,17). Sabbath was not imposed on the Gentiles, but Sunday-keeping originated in Gentile communities.

Bacchiocchi traces the exclusive observance of Sunday to the time of Emperor Hadrian (117-138), when Roman anti-Jewish repression necessitated a policy of deliberate differentiation from Jewish customs.

The only examples in the New Testament of a first-day

meeting prove to be Saturday evening rather than Sunday morning. In Jewish thinking, a new day begins at sundown. Thus in Acts 20:7, Paul preached all night and left on Sunday morning. He did not take a day of rest and worship on Sunday.

At any rate, there is no biblical evidence which suggests that Sabbath does not have its value as a sign of God's continued covenant with Israel originally made with Abraham. For a *Messianic Jew it is a day which celebrates the Sabbath rest which is ours in Yeshua, Lord of the Sabbath.*

Messianic Jews must avoid a legalistic approach to Sabbath where rules are imposed ad infinitum. At the same time, if Sabbath is to be taken seriously, there are some basic principles which should be applied.

First of all, Sabbath should be a day of freedom from work, especially work required for our economic and material security. Judaism has always recognized that professions requiring help in emergencies are exceptions (e.g., doctors, nurses, firemen). Even these people however, need renewal and should seek a period of rest sometime.

Secondly, it is of value to mark the day off from other days by a special Friday evening meal, the lighting of candles, and prayer. This makes us conscious of entering into a special period of time. Some Messianic Jews bring special recognition to Yeshua, who is the light of the world, in their Friday evening Shabbat meal. Blessings over bread and wine for Sabbath are also good.

Sabbath is an appropriate day to gather for worship and hear the Word exposited. It is a time also for fellowship with family and friends. It is a wonderful time for restful, quiet activities we might otherwise overlook. Reading biblical stories together, quiet games, sharing with friends, even just napping, can all be interwoven to make Sabbath a joy. The Sabbath also may be ended with special prayer. The Havdalah service is a meaningful way of doing this. Havdalah means a separation from Sabbath. A special candle is lit and extinguished in wine. Sweet spices are shaken in a spice box and sniffed by all as a reminder of the sweetness of Sabbath, a fragrance of beauty. Some will recognize that we have chosen traditional (rabbinic) practices that are in keeping with the Spirit of the New Covenant and the beauty and joy that is our inheritance.

What is of primary importance is that our activity to be a true renewal of life in God. We need not legalistically define what constitutes work. However, activity which is wearing on us, which depresses, which is related to material security, is to be avoided. The rule of the New Testament is to engage in activity that is spiritually renewing or redemptive for ourselves or others. Sabbath should be a *real contrast* from other work days. Congregations with Sabbath schedules ought to be careful they do not tax their people with too much activity. To make Sabbath a delight, our celebration should be creatively expressed, not rote.

(Much material on Sabbath is available from Jewish publishers. *The Jewish Catalogue* is a fine source for facts about all the holidays.)

PASSOVER

Passover is the great feast which recalls the Exodus from Egyptian bondage. It celebrates the birth of Israel as a nation in freedom. Passover is a feast without equal. It is full of meanings which relate to all followers of Messiah. The Exodus is a type or image pattern of all of God's redemptive acts, even of the final redemption and the establishment of God's Kingdom. Passover involves these salient facts:

1. The slaughter of the Passover lamb and the placing of its blood on the doorpost and on the lintel, is used in the New Testament as the background for understanding the death of Yeshua. As the angel of death *passed-over* the houses of the Israelites who were protected by the blood of the lamb, even so we are passed from death unto life by the atonement blood of Yeshua. Thus Yeshua died on Passover because He is "our Passover lamb" who was slain (John 19, I Corinthians 5:6ff). We are cautioned:

> "Your boasting is not good. Don't you know that a little yeast works through the whole batch of dough? Get rid of the old yeast that you may be a new batch without yeast—as you really are. For Messiah, our Passover lamb, has been sacrificed. Therefore let us

keep the Festival, not the old yeast, the yeast of malice and wickedness, but with bread without yeast, the
bread of sincerity and truth." (I Corinthians 5:6-8)

Leaven was not eaten by Israel when they left Egypt
because the dough had no time to rise. Leaven became a symbol
of that indwelling evil which pervades and affects life. Thus
*Passover symbolism is central to Paul's exposition of the mean-
ing of Mssiah Yeshua.*

2. In the New Testament, 5,000 Israelites ate loaves multi-
plied by the supernatural power of God, in Yeshua. The feeding
of the 5,000 reflects the Passover symbolism of the manna in the
wilderness.

3. The early believers, *both* Jew and Gentile, celebrated
the resurrection of the Messiah during Passover which began
the eight-day feast of unleavened bread. Yeshua had replaced
the sacrificial lamb, which became absent in the celebration.

4. The Messiah's memorial meal (the Last Supper), was a
Passover meal in which Yeshua made the wine of the cup of
redemption (third cup), and the bread of the Afikoman (des-
sert), symbolize His broken body and shed blood. He was telling
His disciples to make the bread and wine of the Passover meal a
symbol of His redemption and partaking a participation in its
power and meaning.

In the light of this we can see how Passover is celebrated by
Messianic Jews. They of course rejoice in the eight-day festival,
and give thanksgiving to God for their redemption from Egyptian bondage, their birth as a nation, and their continued preservation. Eating only unleavened bread for eight days, having
special services, and the Passover meal itself on the 15th day of
Nisan, is a joyous part of their celebration. However, their
celebration incorporates all of the meanings of Yeshua's life in
us. The bread and wine stand for Him. He is seen in all of the
sacrificial images which are part of Passover.

This is a great teaching time for the family. The family and
its guests gather for the meal on the 15th of Nisan. Each family
has a Seder (order) or Passover meal, reading the stories of the
Exodus and our redemption in Yeshua. The festival is an eight-
day celebration of the resurrection, with special days off from

work to gather as a congregation on the first and seventh days as enjoined in Leviticus 23.

Passover is a special celebration of God's grace in both Old and New Testament times. We should note that we believe the proscription of guests who are not circumcised from the meal is not applicable to any believer who is clean (circumcised in heart) in Yeshua (Acts 10).

Passover celebrates the fulfillment of God's promise to Abraham to make him a great nation and to bring Messiah from his seed. There is no legalism involved in this joyous celebration. Thousands of Messianic Jews around the world celebrate Passover.

FIRSTFRUITS—COUNTING THE OMER

In Leviticus 23:9-14, we read about the feast of Firstfruits celebrated on the Sabbath after Passover. The feast includes offering to God the first of the produce of the year. As we said earlier, in this age, Yeshua the Messiah takes the place of all the sacrificial dimensions of all the feasts. Although this feast is not as major in Scripture as other feasts, it does have important significance. For us it is a celebration of the resurrection because we read in I Corinthians 15:20,22b, "But Messiah has indeed been raised from the dead, the firstfruits of those who have fallen asleep . . . so in Messiah all will be made alive."

The meaning of firstfruits is the promise of more to come. Because Yeshua rose from the dead, there is more to come, namely the resurrection of all His followers. We recommend the following as part of Messianic Jewish practice: A gathering for worship, either by congregation or families, to read Leviticus 23:9-14 and I Corinthians 15 on the resurrection; a special offering given to our congregations or other worthy spiritual ministries to show that all we have is God's.

In ancient Israel, Firstfruits celebrated the beginning of the barley harvest. In remembering this feast, we tie ourselves to our people and its land.

SHAVUOTH (WEEKS)—PENTECOST (50)

We are told to count 49 days or seven weeks after Firstfruits to the feast of Shavuoth. These days are actually counted in synagogues in Jewish liturgy. This is called the "counting of the Omer." The fiftieth day is the celebration of Shavuoth, one of the three major festivals at which males presented themselves before God at Jerusalem.

In biblical times Shavuoth originally signified thanksgiving for the first harvest of wheat. However, by Yeshua's time, this ancient feast was connected by Rabbinic calculation to the time God gave the revelation on Sinai. It is of value to connect ourselves to the land by this feast, as well as celebrate the giving of the law in our worship.

However, beyond all of this there is a central meaning for Messianic Jews and Christians who have adopted this holiday. For it was on this day God sovereignly chose to give the Holy Spirit (Ruach ha Kodesh) to Yeshua's gathered followers. In Acts 2 we have the marvelous story of how they preached the gospel supernaturally to Jewish people from many lands in many languages. The followers of Yeshua were able to preach in these languages they had never learned, the wonderful languages they had never learned, the wonderful news of salvation. A great harvest of people were gathered into the new community of faith on this day.

How significant it is that God providentially gave His Spirit on this day, because only through the power of the Spirit can we do God's will. It is by the Spirit that God's law is written on our hearts (Ezekiel 36, Hebrews 10:16).

Shavouth is thus a celebration of all of these biblical meanings and events. It is a day of rest and worship. Homes and congregational buildings may be decorated with greens. The services of worship, at home and in congregations, emphasize the truths of the relationship of the law of God and the Spirit of God who inspired the writing of the law. Special gifts to worthy ministries and needy people are also ways of showing gratitude to God at this time. It is also an ideal time to recommit ourselves to walk in the Spirit.

ROSH HASHANAH

The Feast of Trumpets, the New Year. This holy day takes place in the autumn on the first of Tishri in the Jewish calendar. Originally this day was not celebrated as a new year, but Rabbinic calculation fixed the anniversary of the creation of man to this day.

Actually, Israel was originally to observe this day as the day of blowing of the shofar (ram's horn) in preparation for Yom Kippur. Thus Jewish tradition rightly incorporates prayers seeking forgiveness on this day, as well as new-year memorials. Scripturally, our people were told to celebrate the month of the feast of Passover as their new year. Tishri was actually the new-year festival of the surrounding nations of the Near East, just as January first is our New Year's Day. There is nothing wrong with also remembering the creation of the world on this day, as long as we do not lose sight of it being an entrance into the days of self-examination and repentance before God.

The Feast of Trumpets also reminds us of the return of Yeshua the Messiah to rule and reign. It says in I Thessalonians 4:16-19,

> "For the Lord Himself will come down from heaven, with a loud command, with the voice of the archangel and with the shofar of God, and the dead in Messiah will rise first. After that, we who are still alive and are left will be caught up with them in the clouds . . . and so we will be with the Lord forever . . . therefore encourage each other with these words."

We also read in I Corinthians 15 that we shall be changed in a moment at the resurrection, at the *last shofar*, in the twinkling of an eye.

Therefore, Messianic Jews celebrate Rosh Hashanah as a day of rest, with services of worship emphasizing preparation for Yom Kippur. Traditional and modern worship material may be creatively adapted to this end.

YOM KIPPUR (The Day of Atonement)

Yom Kippur is the holiest day of the Jewish calendar. In ancient Israel, Yom Kippur was the day on which atonement was made for the whole nation (Leviticus 16). On this day, the high priest went into the Holy of Holies with the sacrificial blood to make atonement for the people's sins. He sprinkled the blood on the Ark of the Covenant.

Yom Kippur also involved the ceremony of the scapegoat. The priest laid his hands on the head of the animal which then symbolically carried away the sins of the people. This was the only day in Torah specified as a day of fasting. On this day the nation was to afflict itself, in repentance for sin. Traditional Judaism incorporates many great prayers of repentance for the seeking of forgiveness, some of which are fraught with Messianic significance.

For example, the merit of the Messiah is appealed to for forgiveness. Forgiveness in traditional Judaism is also asked on the basis of Abraham's offering of Isaac as a sacrifice. Messianic Jews know this to be a foreshadowing of the sacrifice of the Messiah Yeshua. (This is the case in daily services as well.)

Yom Kippur has continued significance in Messianic Judaism. It is not that we seek atonement through our prayers or by the observance of a day, because we know Yeshua the Messiah is our high priest, our atonement, and our scapegoat. The central chapters of the book of Hebrews, which explicate the meaning of Yeshua in the light of Yom Kippur, are central to us on this day.

Yom Kippur is for us a day incorporating these meanings:

1. It is a celebration of the fulfillment of the meaning of priest and sacrifice in Yeshua.
2. It is a day of prayer, fasting, and intercession for Israel, our people.
3. It is a day of self-examination and turning from sin in our lives.

Scripture enjoins us to, "examine ourselves" (I Corinthians 1). I John 1:8,9 says, "If we claim to be without sin, we deceive ourselves and the truth is not in us. If we confess our sins, He is faithful and just and will forgive us our sins and purify us from all unrighteousness."

Yom Kippur is a day to worship in community as well as to

be apart, to take stock of the direction of our life over the past year. Where have we missed God's best direction? Where have we grown? Where have we slipped? As James 4 enjoins us, we repent, or turn from these sins unto God. It is true that confession and forgiveness are to form a daily part of our lives in Yeshua, however, as individuals and as a community, it is of value to have a special season for this purpose as well.

The services for Yom Kippur emphasize Messianic fulfillment as well as all of the above elements. The break fast is a special time of rejoicing and celebration for our forgiveness in Yeshua.

Two areas of special misunderstanding are worth noting about Yom Kippur. One is the "Kol Nidre" (All Vows), the chant which begins the first evening service called the Kol Nidre service. This chant asks forgiveness for all past and future vows which shall be broken. It is not that Jewish people intended to break vows they made, but at times under extreme duress and torture, Jews were forced to make vows which they could not keep in loyalty to God. This prayer became a paradigm of the nature of our need for forgiveness in all areas of life. The prayer does not seek a blank check for us to sin and yet be forgiven. Rather it reflects human weakness in persecution.

Secondly, both Hashanah and Yom Kippur services pray for us to be inscribed in the Book of Life (for the coming year). Followers of Yeshua sometimes have difficulty with both the prayer and the Rosh Hashanah greeting: "May you be inscribed."

The Book of Life may refer to several books within Judaism. However, some think the reference is to the symbolic book of eternal life found in the book of Revelation. Some references to the Book of Life, however, are in the sense of God's decrees concerning those who will be kept in life and health for the coming year. In this sense there is no problem with the greeting or the prayer. Regardless, the Holy Days are of great significance for Messianic Jews.

STUDY QUESTIONS

1. Why do we argue that the feasts of Israel are bound up with

   the Abrahamic Covenant? _____

   _____

   _____

   _____

   _____

2. Name and define the major feasts.

   a. S _____

   _____

   b. P _____

   _____

   c. S _____

   _____

   d. S _____

   _____

3. List several central dimensions of the meaning of Sabbath.

   a. _____

   _____

   b. _____

   _____

c. _____

_____

d. _____

_____

4. Yeshua never did away with the Sabbath but He had prob-

lems with legalism. Explain. _____

_____

_____

_____

5. What was Paul's practice in regard to non-Jews and the
Sabbath? How does this relate to Jews?

_____

_____

_____

6. Summarize the meaning of Passover in two parts: a) the
original event in history and, b) its meaning in Yeshua.

a. _____

_____

_____

b. _____

_____

_____

7. What is Firstfruits? _____

_____

_____

_____

8. What is the meaning of Shavouth? Include its meaning in

   fulfilled form. _____

_____

_____

_____

_____

9. How does a Messianic Jew relate to Yom Kippur? _____

_____

_____

_____

_____

VERSES FOR MEMORIZATION

Review all verses previously assigned.
I Corinthians 5:7,8

SUKKOTH (Booths or Tabernacles)

Soon after Yom Kippur the feast of Sukkoth begins. It is the third major feast in which the males of Israel traveled to Jerusalem. Sukkoth is an eight-day festival during which the people of Israel were to dwell in tents to recall their wilderness wanderings. During the wilderness period, the people of Israel had little in the way of possessions, no permanent dwellings and little natural provision for food. Yet God supernaturally provided for their needs for food, clothing and shelter. When they had almost nothing, God provided.

Dwelling in tents was to be a vivid reminder of God's grace. The Israelites were to remember that although they might have homes, land, and other measures of wealth, their lives were still just as dependent upon God. Security was not to be found in possessions. Nor was Israel to think that her might or wealth was a product of her self-righteousness or power (Deuteronomy 8-10). Israel was to love and trust God first and only. The eight-day celebration of booths is a vivid reminder of these truths.

The feast of Sukkoth was also a celebration of the last major harvest period in Israel. It was a great festival of thanksgiving. Part of the tradition of this feast is the recitation of the Hallel Psalms 113-118 and the waving of fruit (etrog) and branches of palm and willow (lulav) before God (Leviticus 23).

Hospitality is also an essential part of observing Sukkoth. In gratitude for God's provision, we share with others. The first and eighth day of the festival are assemblies of worship.

The feast of Tabernacles is also full of Messianic significance. In John 7 through 9, Yeshua's teaching is better understood in the context of the feast of Sukkoth. The last day of Sukkoth was the context of His statement: "If anyone thirst let him come to Me and drink. He who believes in Me as the Scripture has said, out of his heart shall flow rivers of living water." He said this about the Spirit.

We know from the description of Sukkoth in the Talmud that this was the day in which a great ceremony of pouring out waters of libation took place.

The joyful ceremony of the festival reached its climax in Temple times when the procedure known as "the joy of water drawing" began on the second night of Sukkoth and lasted for six days. Each morning a libation offering of water was made. It was taken in a golden ewer from the pool of Siloam, carried with great pomp and ceremony, and poured into a perforated silver bowl placed on the west side of the altar, symbolizing the abundant rain for which the people prayed. Bonfires were lit and men of piety danced, holding torches and singing songs and hymns to the accompaniment of harps, lyres, cymbals, and trumpets played by Levites.

During the last day of the feast there was a magnificent lamp-lighting ceremony in the court of the women. The Temple shone with an incredible brightness of light. This was in all probability the context of Yeshua's statement, "I am the Light of the world. Whoever follows Me will never walk in darkness, but will have the Light of life." (John 8:12).

Matthew 6 is an excellent chapter to remember at Sukkoth time for it supremely recounts the nature of God's fatherly care.

How is Sukkoth best celebrated by Messianic Jews? There are a variety of creative ways to celebrate Sukkoth. First, as in all the feasts, the sacrificial dimensions are replaced by Yeshua's sacrifice. In addition, services on the first and last days of Sukkoth are a time for the gathered community to give thanks, wave fruit and branches in thanksgiving, read the Hallel Psalms 113-118, and creatively worship using traditional and modern material. Evenings should be times of special fellowship through the sharing of meals and reading of the Scriptures we have mentioned.

One question, of course, relates to the biblical stipulation to dwell in tents. In Israel, with a warm climate, the practice is not only beautiful, but practical. Realizing this, the Rabbis have tried to instill the practice of building a Sukkah and at least taking meals in it.

As we look at Messianic Jewish practice we see the importance of conveying the meaning of this feast in an enjoyable way, recognizing that the command to dwell in booths was given for the nation dwelling in its land, possessing its land, houses, and security. In the diaspora, there is a great measure of freedom. Climate permitting, we indeed recommend the building of a Sukkah by families and eating meals in it. Decorating the Sukkah is a great joy to children, a festive spirit prevails.

Some Messianic Jews try to take a camping trip during part of Sukkoth so they get a greater sense of having just the bare necessities and of God's provision for us through the produce of the land.

The first and last days of the eight-day festival are special days of rest and community gathering for worship celebration. Traditionally, this was also a period of looking forward to the Messianic kingdom. God someday will be seen as the provider for all the earth, thus this feast will be universally observed, according to Zechariah 14. All nations will send representatives to Jerusalem to observe this feast with Israel. May God speed the day of the coming of His Kingdom! In this way Sukkoth awaits a future time of fulfillment as well.

MINOR FEASTS AND FASTS
(Not an exhaustive list)

A. *Simhat Torah* (Rejoicing of the Torah)

Since we have just described Sukkoth, it is fitting we describe Simhat Torah. Simhat Torah is not a biblically prescribed feast. It occurs immediately after Sukkoth and celebrates the transition from the last reading of the annual Torah reading cycle, to the first reading of the annual cycle. The Jewish community created a great festival of joy on the day which could have been merely a day of tedious rerolling of the communities' scrolls from end to beginning. We might ask, is it not also a great cause for rejoicing to complete a reading of the Scriptures by the community and the opportunity to begin reading again?

The festival includes music and dancing with the Torah scrolls. Among women of the Orthodox Hasidic communities the celebration soars into great heights of joy and energy. Among Messianic Jews there is further cause of rejoicing because in the Messiah we are accounted righteous and have the joy of God's Torah written on our hearts by His Spirit.

B. *Purim*

This celebrates the deliverance of Israel from a wicked plot of annihilation during the days of the Persian empire. The book of Esther records the account of the wicked plot of Haman and the efforts of Queen Esther (Hadassah) to influence the king to save her people. Purim falls near the end of winter in the month of Adar. It is characterized by plays, songs, costumes, and the reading of the scroll of Esther (the megillah) during which children make noise with groggers to drown out the name of Haman. Other great periods of danger and deliverance in Israel's history are also remembered at this time. The creative possibilities for Messianic Jewish celebration of this day are unlimited.

C. *Yom Ha Sho'ah*—Day of Calamity

This day, occurring in the Spring on the 25th of Nisan, recalls the destruction of European Jewry under the unspeakable horrors of the Nazis. The day is marked by both synagogues and larger communities by services which include memorial prayers, reading from concentration camp poetry and literature, and recommitment to the survival of Israel. Messianic Jews join in mourning and memory with the whole community on this day, as well as affirming the ultimate hope of justice and peace in the reign of the Messiah.

Lutheran Franklin Litiell suggests a service for Christian churches in his book, *The Crucifixion of the Jews*. Having this service would indicate the Church's repentance for its silence in the face of this atrocity. At the same time it would be showing a solidarity of mourning and memory with the Jewish community.

D. *Israel's Independence Day* (Yom Ha Atzma'ut)

In the spring on the 5th of Iyar is the day which marks the rebirth of the state of Israel in 1948. It is a day of prophetic fulfillment and celebration. Congregations and communities all over the world celebrate this miracle!

E. *Tisha B'Av* (The Ninth of Av)

This day, which occurs in mid-summer, is a day of fasting

and sadness. For on this day, supernaturally by any standard of unbiased reasoning, the first Temple of Israel was destroyed in 586 B.C.E. by the Babylonians and the second was destroyed in 70 C.E. by Titus. Incredibly as it seems, both were destroyed on the same date 656 years apart. Also, the decree of the expulsion of the Jewish community from Spain in 1492 went into effect on this day.

Messianic Jews on this day should seek identity with their people, mourning in prayer intercession while reflecting on such judgments. We can read passages of comfort and hope in the Scripture and pray for the peace of Jerusalem as well as the salvation of friends and all of Israel. Oh, that there would be a full return to God through the Messiah Yeshua.

F. *Chanukah*—The Feast of Dedication

This feast celebrates the amazing victories in Israel's overthrow of its tyrannical Syrio-Greek rulers during the days of the Maccabees. The Syrio-Greek Empire sought not only to rule Israel, but to destroy its unique religious fidelity to Scripture. They imposed pagan customs and rites on Israel, even in the Temple itself. Many Jews were martyred for their faith. Thus in the 160s B.C.E., the Maccabee family led a great revolt, eventually culminating in the rededication of the Temple and the independence of Israel for the first time in over 400 years.

Chanukah itself, which usually falls in early winter on the 25th of Kislev, marks the rededication of the temple. During the eight-day festival the candles of an eight-branched Menorah are lit. Each day one more candle is lit. This recalls the reported miracle of oil for one day, but the light burned for eight days until new oil could be obtained.

Messianic Jews celebrate the victories of those days with the rest of the Jewish community. They retell the stories of Chanukah from the books of the Maccabees as well as reliving these events through Chanukah plays. Messianic Jews should also recall that this feast was the occasion of Yeshua's profound teaching on the relationship between Himself, as the good shepherd, and the rest of His sheep, who "hear His voice," know Him, and follow Him (John 10).

We must not overlook the fact that it is in a similar time

frame that most Christians celebrate Christmas. Although there is no ambivalence among Messianic Jews about the biblical meaning of Christmas as the time of Messiah Yeshua's entrance into this world, Christmas itself brings ambivalent feeling to many Messianic Jews. Why is this?

First of all, scholars usually hold this date is not the time of the Messiah's birth. Usually, the date is explained as one which correlates to the older winter solstice festival in which pagans symbolically sought to magically assure the resurrection of spring. Perhaps the reason for the Church's choice of this date was to counter such paganism with a Christian holiday. But the ambivalence persists. The Puritan Christians forbade the celebration of Christmas in the 16th and 17th centuries because of supposed pagan connections.

The Jewish community has tended to emphasize Chanukah, which was a more minor feast, to counter the influence of Christmas by having a parallel holiday with gift-giving. Recently Cardinal Jean Danilou proposed the idea that the reason December 25th (a solar calendar date) could be proposed as a date for the birth of the Messiah, in the light of its pagan connections, is found that in the fact that the 25th of Chislev (a lunar calendar date) already possessed great significance to Messianic Jews. Danilou argues this was originally the celebration of the birth of James, the brother of Yeshua. In later times this connection was lost and the 25th of Chislev became identified with the 25th of December and the birth of Yeshua.

Is there a solution to the problem of these dates and the ambivalence they cause? A solution which meets the special need to recognize Yeshua's birth, as well as reading with special festivity the passages that so profoundly record the details of His birth (Matthew 1,2; Luke 1,2)?

If we look at the practice of Messianic Jews of today and yesteryear, in celebrating the resurrection of Yeshua, we might find a solution. Messianic Jews celebrate the resurrection in connection with the 15th of Nisan, which is Passover. Thus they follow the Jewish lunar calendar for religious observances. Although there is no agreement on the date of Messiah's birth, perhaps we can make some creative new suggestions.

Without Chanukah and the preservation of the Jewish

community by God, Yeshua would never have come. Chanukah is a festival of lights and Yeshua is the Light of the world.
Perhaps then for Messianic Jews the climax of Chanukah can
be the celebration of the birth of Yeshua. However, this celebration, by the Jewish lunar date, is the 25th of Chislev. It is
well then to read the birth narratives. Also, during Chanukah,
the life of James, the great leader of the Messianic Jewish
community in Jerusalem, can be recalled. Messianic Jews need
to produce storybooks and celebration ideas incorporating all
these significant events in the light of Yeshua. These books
would be of help to both families and congregations. This is only
a suggestion, but it is put forth with the hope it has some merit.

OTHER COMMON WORSHIP PRACTICES

The Tzitzit (Fringes)
    "The Lord said to Moses, 'Speak to the Israelites
    and say to them: Throughout the generations to come
    you are to make tassels on the corners of your gar-
    ments, with a blue cord on each tassel. You will have
    these tassels to look at and so you will remember all
    the commands of the Lord, that you may obey them
    and not prostitute yourselves by going after the lusts
    of your own hearts and eyes. Then you will remember
    to obey all My commands and will be consecrated to
    your God. I am the Lord your God. . . .' " (Numbers
    15:37-41)

The meaning of this command is quite simple. The ancient
Israelites wore four-cornered garments, almost like a sheet
with cut-outs for head and arms. On each corner of the garment
was to be sewn a fringe or tassel with a cord of blue. (This is not
sure because biblical words for colors are very uncertain.) The
cord of blue was to be a reminder to do all in commitment to
God, not out of selfish desire, but to be consecrated to God and
obey all His commands. Whenever the cord was looked upon, it
was to recall the Israelite to his commitment.
    Our desire as Messianic Jews is to recapture the *spirit* (the
reason and application for today) of the law, not just the letter.

This command does not mean that we as western, 20th century people must return to the dress of 3,500 years ago and sew tassels on the corners of our garments. But it does mean we should seek ways to constantly remind ourselves of our commitment to God and His commandments, that the love of God will be constantly remembered.

Messianic Jews may find value in the prayer shawl, a garment developed for the purpose of keeping this command. As they place the prayer shawl upon themselves, they return to their first love, Yeshua. Some Messianic Jews find value in wearing the tallit katan under their shirt so that fringes are worn in all their waking hours. We must also recall the words of Yeshua, "If you love Me, keep My commandments." The fringes still have value, however, it is the principle of memory which is important, not enforcing a particular means of memory.

Yeshua wore the fringes, and those who sought healing from Him would try to touch them (Mark 5:28, 6:56). Some people also use the tallit as a symbol of being clothed with the righteousness of Yeshua in whom we are accounted righteous. By His power in us we fulfill God's commands.

H.L. Ellison argues that Paul certainly wore fringes all of the time or he would not have been listened to in the synagogue.*

Tefillin—Phylacteries

In Deuteronomy 6:4-9 ("The Shema Passage"), we read, "Love the Lord your God with all your heart and with all your soul and with all your strength," and that these words should be tied "as symbols on your hands and bind them on your foreheads. Write them on the doorframes of your houses and on your gates" as well.

The traditional means for fulfilling this command is a small box with leather straps which is placed on the arm, the straps being woven around the arm and hand. Another box with leather straps is placed upon the head. The command in relation to gates and doorposts is fulfilled through use of the Mezuzah, a small container affixed in the proper place on the

---

* In Gasque and Martin, *Apostolic History and The Gospel.*

door. All three contain biblical verses enjoined by Scripture. The *tefillin* is worn daily in daytime prayer services.

Again we have a significant memory device in Scripture. Jewish tradition rejects the use of tefillin on Sabbath because Sabbath is also called a "sign" between God and Israel of God's covenant relation with Israel. Jewish reasoning eschews the use of signs in any way that one sign could detract from the significance of the other; the tefillin are also taken to be a covenant sign.

The spirit of the law allows freedom in the usage of these memory practices and emphasizes the memory purpose of the commands. Perhaps a modern rendition would be to write the shema on our dashboards so we remember it while driving to work, or place it in other visible spots (e.g., the bathroom mirror while shaving). However, the Mezuzah is a good and simple memory device which adds Jewish character to a home.

The foreignness of tefillin to many modern Jews should not cause us to discount it as a meaningful way to worship when done in heartfelt gratitude to God. Indeed, learning to affix the tefillin in morning prayer can be a real joy whereby physical gestures become a part of worship, too. However, we are also strictly warned not to make any sign an ostentatious display to call attention to ourselves (Matthew 23:5,6; 6:5-18).

Biblical Food and Cleanliness Laws (Leviticus 11-16; Deuteronomy 14)

It is a difficult task to understand the food and cleanliness laws of these chapters. There are many possiblilities of interpretation. *There is a health explanation* used by Elmer Josephson in, *God's Key to Health and Happiness*, and many other publications. This explanation holds that the avoidance of the foods on these lists prevented disease since the various animals forbidden as unclean were dangerous for human consumption. The ban against touching dead bodies, animals, and the rule of uncleanness in regards to issues of blood, leprosy, and emissions of all kinds, are interpreted as safeguards aganst possible disease.

Some animals on the list in these chapters are known today

to have adverse health effects. Some people argue that even the
best preparation of pork does not prevent trichinosis. However,
although God's stipulations here do have a connection with
health, one has to stretch a bit far to find health reasons for
every rule. Why, for example, is a woman unclean only 33 days
after giving birth to a male, but 66 days after giving birth to a
female? Other laws in the list are also problematic. Why is one
unclean after sexual intercourse?

A second explanation, still widely held, was given great
scholarly support in the *Old Testament Commentary* of Keil
and Deiletch. They argued that the clean and unclean distinctions were symbolic reminders of sin. Since death entered the
world through sin, all those born since Adam were transgressors, all things connected with birth and death render one
unclean.

Unclean animals were scavengers, they feed off of death.
Touching that which is dead is an intimate contact with "the
wages of sin." Sexual intercourse is itself not sinful, but is the
means of perpetuating a race which is fallen, although in the
light of redemption such perpetuation is desirable. In addition,
birth falls under the same symbol of making unclean. Leprosy
is symbolic of the indwelling sin nature. Other disease condi-
tions also reflect sin and render one unclean. The woman
sinned first, so the 66-day period of uncleanness is a reminder of
this fact, while the 33-day period reminds us of Adam's sin.

*A third explanation is that of Mary Douglas, who holds that
the lists reflect something of a distinction between the ancient
ideas of wholeness and fit, and that which did not fit and was
therefore abhorrent.* Thus fish have scales, but that which is
like a fish, but lacks scales, lacks in wholeness.

Perhaps these explanations for the clean-unclean distinctions and the forbidden food lists all have some value. The
evidence is certainly not so clear as to justify dogmatism. We
should note, however, that the unclean person was in some
cases isolated, a clear disease preventative, and was *forbidden
during the specified period from participation in the Temple
and its sacrificial system.* This system was to reflect purity,
holiness, and the wholeness of redemption. One could be

unclean till evening, and then take a special bath and become clean, or unclean seven days or for the duration of the disease. In some aspects, therefore, the clean-unclean distinctions are for the age of the Temple which was replaced for us in Yeshua.

Still, the health dimensions and Jewish identification dimensions of these lists may be taken seriously by Messianic Jews. Many Christians avoid the foods on the forbidden lists of Scripture. To avoid such foods and practice good hygiene makes good sense. For Americans it would mostly involve avoiding pork and shellfish, the only two main American foods on the list, as well as the eating of blood. Messianic Jews who practice these principles say they follow biblical Kashrut (Kosher). Not eating blood was commanded to Noah (Gen 9) and is universally binding on the human race.

THE IMPORTANCE OF
MESSIANIC JEWISH CONGREGATIONS

Some of you having read this far, may conclude with us it is valid and expedient for Messianic Jews to maintain their Jewish identity and practice. You may, however, question why it is important for Messianic Jews to form congregations. Isn't is possible for Messianic Jews to be part of non-Jewish New Testament fellowships and still maintain their individual and family Jewish identity, as well as their involvement in the Jewish community? Yes, it is possible. There are some strong individuals who have done this, even maintaining regular synagogue attendance. We do not want to dissuade these people from their patterns, but want to invite them to weigh their stance in terms of effectiveness for God's kingdom.

For most people such a strong individual stance is simply not practical. Messianic congregations can provide many necessary functions for God's kingdom. They provide a *unique corporate witness of the Messiahship of Yeshua to the Jewish community. They are the most forceful and visible testimony that Jewish believers have not forsaken their love of Israel, because their lifestyle and worship are Jewish. They also testify by the presence of non-Jewish members that Jew and Gentile are one in the Messiah.*

In addition, Messianic congregations are able to *provide for the unique ongoing discipleship needs of Jewish believers wrestling with the questions of their Jewish identity and practice and the New Testament faith.*

The Messianic congregation can provide the worship, social, and educational context for raising children of Jewish New Testament believers as Messianic Jews, with a strong and secure identity in Yeshua. Messianic Jewish congregations also provide *the practical means of an ongoing and growing lay witness for Yeshua in the Jewish community.*

For most people, it is simply too difficult to give adequate time to their Jewish heritage and Jewish community involvements, as well as to be adequately involved in a non-Jewish congregation. But in a Messianic congregation one is in the universal body and his involvement dovetails with his call as a Jew. The eventual end of many not in a Messianic congregation is slippage for a Jewish life, which results in a good chance of assimilation by the children of these Jewish believers.

Many Jewish practices are congregational in nature. The only model, other than the Messianic Jewish congregation, which is practical is a congregation which is not Jewish but has a group of Messianic Jews who are encouraged to maintain a Jewish life. There are some churches who are open to this and have encouraged their Jewish members in this way. Some Jews would not respond to this very well though since one of the accusations against Jewish believers has been that they are not self-supporting and are a missionary arm or front for a non-Jewish group. However, we must never for this reason deny our oneness with all believers and the validity of the second model.

Recent studies in missiology have shown that the greatest potential for the spreading of the gospel is the planting of indigenous congregations adapted to the culture of the people they seek to reach. If such indigenous congregations have a strong emphasis on witnessing and discipleship, they are far and away the most effective means of spreading the Kingdom. The biblical method of spreading the gospel was just this, the planting of congregations which were able to adapt to the needs of the cultural communities in which they were planted.

LIFE IN A MESSIANIC CONGREGATION

A Messianic congregation is involved in all the tasks of any truly biblical congregation. It seeks to provide a congregational home of fellowship for its members. This congregational home should be a central focus of the commitment of each member. Indeed, the questions of where we live, work, and how we spend our time and money, should be related to our primary involvement in the congregation. We are to seek to become one in love, fellowship, and mutual ministry. Secondly, we need to use our gifts to build up the body. We applaud the nationwide movement of believers to live in proximity to one another and share their lives more deeply on a day-to-day basis.

Additionally, congregations need to be witnesses of our faith through the quality of life in the community of faith. We must disciple others in the Scriptures, as well as find the best means of spreading the Good News.

The congregational tasks of education, worship, service, preaching, and counseling, are those of a Messianic congregation as well. Indeed, the Messianic congregation must provide the full means of healing and growth which is part of biblical congregational life. The means for physical healing, inner healing, freedom from oppression, the Messiah's memorial, and the Mikvah of Yeshua (baptism), are all part of congregational life.

We believe very deeply that life in the body, with the operation of the ministry gifts of the Spirit through love (I Corinthians 12-14), is a means of growth which a believer in Yeshua may not forego. Congregational life is the means by which God encourages, corrects, and enables us to grow into maturity, to be like the Messiah. Elder-leadership in congregational life is necessary as well, to give the congregation direction from the Lord. Within the bounds of Scriptural truth, we are called to be accountable to one another and to our leaders (Hebrews 13:7,17; I Peter 5). Thus elder insight and counsel are also a crucial part of our growth and decision-making.

STUDY QUESTIONS

1. How would a Messianic Jew celebrate Sukkoth? _____

_____

_____

_____

2. What is Simhat Torah? _____

_____

_____

3. What is Purim? _____

_____

_____

_____

4. What is Yom Ha Sho'ah? _____

_____

_____

_____

5. What is Tisha B'Av? _____

_____

_____

6. What is the meaning of Chanukah? _____

_____

_____

7. What are tzitzit and tefillin? _____

_____

_____

8. Give three explanations for the clean-unclean food distinctions in the Torah.

   a. _____

     _____

   b. _____

     _____

   c. _____

     _____

9. Give four reasons for the importance of Messianic Jewish congregations.

   a. _____

     _____

   b. _____

     _____

c. _____

_____

d. _____

_____

IMPORTANT ISSUES

VIII—IMPORTANT ISSUES

SECTION A—JUDAISM AND CHRISTIANITY

HISTORY

In this section we want to give some understanding to the historical split between the church and the synagogue. Accomplishing this requires a maximum of tact and respect, without compromising honesty. A more complete treatment of this subject is available in my booklet, *Jewishness and Jesus*. Studies are also available in Fr. Edward Flannery's *The Anguish of the Jews*, and in James Parkes' *The Conflict of the Church and the Synagogue*. In this section we will only lay out a very basic summary of history more accurately documented in the mentioned writings.

At the end of the New Testament period, there was basic understanding among the leadership in regard to Jews and Gentiles and the body of believers.

1. With regard to non-Jewish believers, Acts 15 *settled several issues:*

   a. They were to be given freedom from converting to Judaism and taking upon themselves the totality of Jewish lifestyle.
   b. They were to abstain from immorality and other practices which would preclude their fellowship with their Jewish brethren in the faith.
   c. They were, however, to grow in maturity through an

      understanding of the Tenach and by apostolic teaching
      (II Timothy 3:16,17).

   d. They were to respect the heritage of Jewish people to
      the extent it was biblical and consistent with the New
      Covenant order, since this heritage clarified the mean-
      ing of their own faith (Acts 15:21, II Timothy 3:16,17,
      Ephesians 2:20, Romans 11:18,28,29).

2. With regard to Jewish believers, it was assumed and
accepted that they would maintain their Jewish biblical heritage to the extent it was consistent with the New Covenant
order. This would be the case both in predominantly Jewish
New Covenant congregations, such as in Israel, as well as in
diaspora congregations of mixed composition.

   a. This is proven by the testimony of the Jewish leadership
      in Acts 21 and the personal testimony of Paul in his
      faithfulness to the Jewish biblical heritage (Acts 18:18,
      Acts 21:17-26, 28:17).

   b. It is proven by excellent historical evidence on the life of
      James and the other Jewish disciples of Yeshua. It is
      shown as well in sources on the life and practice of the
      disciples from the first into the mid-second century,
      known as the Nazarenes. Sources are found in the Tal-
      mud, Josephus, Heggasippus, Justin Martyr, and Euse-
      bius. (We contrast the Nazarenes to the Ebionites who
      did not accept the whole authority of the Apostles and
      became heretics.)

3. The mainstream Jewish community was alarmed at the
following Messianic Judaism gained within Israel. Bagatti's
archaeological studies estimate the Messianic Jews became a
major force of hundreds of thousands. The Jewish communities' uneasiness with the Messianic Jews brought them into
argument with and sometimes persecution of Jewish followers
of Yeshua but not the Gentile followers.

4. The mainstream Gentile Roman culture persecuted the
followers of Yeshua as an illegal Jewish sect; a dangerous sect
because they would not bow to Caesar as a god.

5. There was already a beginning of Gentile pride against Israel whereby non-Jewish believers considered themselves the total replacement of Israel because she had rejected Yeshua as a nation. Paul countered this argument in Romans 11, but we know these were the attitudes which led to later anti-Jewishness.

The period from 70 to 400 is important for us to understand. The fall of Jerusalem and the passing of leadership in the church to Gentile members was momentous for the Messianic Jewish community. The mainstream Jewish community finally came to a complete rejection of the Messianic community. This was officially declared at the Rabbinical council of Yavneh in the year 90 C.E. The reasons for this were several fold:

    a. The Messianic Jews believed Messiah had come and died a shameful death on the cross. This seemed to contradict Jewish expectations of the external kingdom of peace to come in the Messiah's days, despite Messianic Jewish testimony to the resurrection and *second coming.*

    b. The Messianic Jews brought Gentiles into their communities in the diaspora and accepted them as equals without their converting to a full Jewish lifestyle. This undercut the proselytizing efforts of the synagogue.

    c. The Messianic Jews fled Jerusalem before the Roman siege in obedience to Yeshua's prophecy and command in Matthew 24 and Luke 21. This caused them to be branded as traitors.

    d. In the later Bar Kochbah rebellion against Rome in 130 C.E. the Messianic Jews refused to fight behind Bar Kochbah after he was proclaimed the Messiah. This reinforced their rejection and Bar Kochbah massacred Messianic Jewish communities.

    e. The Rabbinic community attempted to shore up Jewish unity for the sake of survival after 70 C.E. To do so they condemned all other expressions of Judaism: Sadducean, Essenian, and Messianic Judaism.

This caused the Messianic Jews to be isolated from the mainstream Jewish community. At the same time the Messianic Jews were also separated from the mainstream Christian community. The church, under the leadership of non-Jews, interpreted the fall of Jerusalem and later Jewish hardships, as clear expressions of God's judgment and final rejection of Israel. Although there was an element of judgment involved in these events, Paul was clear that Israel was still beloved and called of God as a nation (Romans 11:28,29). In spite of this the church made these responses:

1. They interpreted fulfillment as the total elimination of the nation of Israel and the Old Testament order. Fulfillment did not catch up into itself the meanings of the past but was a *break* with the past (cf. O. Cullman, *Salvation History*, and Daniel P. Fuller, *Gospel and Law, Contrast or Continuum*).
2. They interpreted the church as the new Israel, totally replacing national Israel.
3. The church tried not to appear as a Jewish sect to avoid the persecutions of the Jews under Emperor Hadrian.
4. The church tried to supplant pagan traditions by superimposing Christian traditions and meanings on pagan holidays. This was an aid to Christianizing, but made the church appear more pagan and further divided them from Israel. Further replacements for pagan traditions included the saints and Mary as mediators.
5. The church, in light of the above facts, gained an ambivalent attitude to the Old Testament, which in some communities, influenced by Marcion and his heresy, rejected the Old Testament as Scripture. However, more illumined minds prevailed and the church did accept the Old Testament. The ambivalence still remained, though.
6. The church rejected the Messianic Jews because they maintained their Jewish heritage and their belief in the future of Israel. This was officially declared in the Nicean decisions in 325 C.E.

These events created an anti-Jewishness in the church which later led to anti-Semitism. The church's position in relationship to Jewish believers, *until recently*, was that any Jew who accepted Jesus had to renounce Jewish practice, change his name to a Christian name, and eat pork to prove his conversion. At its worst, the institutional church burned Jewish Christians at the stake who engaged in Jewish practice during the Inquisition (circa 1500ff). But today there has been a dramatic, God-ordained change in the church in regard to this. Praise God!

The result was that Messianic Jewish communities were isolated and decimated by wars; the last vestiges were eliminated during the Muslim conquests in the 600's. The church and synagogue lost their bridge of understanding, the Messianic Jews. They increased their opposition to one another. Christianity eventually became the official state religion, leading to economic and social sanctions against the Jews. Anti-Semitism became part of the policy of the state and the institutional church (cf. Parkes).

RECENT HISTORY

Space does not permit even a moderate coverage of this topic. However, we do want to note just a few things. First, as the church and the synagogue hardened their attitudes and arguments, neither could learn from the other. Because the institutional church became a state church, the Jewish rejection of Jesus was used as an excuse for persecution by the state. Of course, people motivated by the love of Messiah don't engage in persecution. However, the devil has his influence even in the church.

The horrors of persecution in the name of Christ are especially seen in the Spanish Inquisition before which all Jews were expelled from Spain. The 19th century pogroms in Eastern Europe and Russia were especially grievous because so many suffered injury and death. The culmination in recent times of anti-Semitism occurred in the horrible holocaust of Adolph Hitler. All the persecutors appealed to the institutional church's theology of Israel, that she was replaced, despised, and worthless.

Yet an amazing change has occurred in recent times, especially in American evangelical churches. Most notable is the theological shift which regards Israel, as a nation, as still playing a significant present and future role in salvation history. The truths of Romans 11 are now clearly affirmed in many sectors of the church. Israel is accepted as elect for the sake of the fathers.

Beyond this, many churches and denominations have taken unequivocal stands against anti-Semitism and in support of Israel's national right to existence. We have experienced an amazing new openness to Jewish believers who maintain their Jewish heritage, as well as desire among Christians to learn the Jewish roots of their faith. To anyone who knows history, these changes appear monumental and without historical precedent. This is a correct assessment.

Of course, we are not saying there are not still problems of anti-Jewish sentiments in some church sectors. Nor are we saying there are not still serious lacks in some places in understanding the Bible's teaching in its Jewish context. What we do affirm is that God's Spirit is producing amazing change and our hearts must be thankful and open to all our brothers and sisters from all denominational backgrounds.

STUDY QUESTIONS

1. The Acts 15 council settled several issues related to non-Jewish believers. List the issues it settled.

   a. _____

   _____

   _____

   b. _____

   _____

   _____

   c. _____

_____

_____

d. _____

_____

_____

2. Summarize the major aspects of the stance early congregations of Yeshua took in regard to the place and life of Jewish
   believers.

a. _____

_____

_____

b. _____

_____

_____

c. _____

_____

_____

3. Give four reasons why the Jewish community leadership
   rejected the Jewish followers of Yeshua.

a. _____

_____

_____

b. _____

_____

_____

c. _____

_____

_____

d. _____

_____

_____

4. Give five reasons why the institutional church rejected Messianic Jews or Nazarenes.

a. _____

_____

_____

b. _____

_____

_____

c. _____

_____

_____

d. _____

_____

_____

e.   _____

_____

_____

5. Summarize the amazing change in recent church history toward Jews and Israel.

_____

_____

_____

_____

_____

_____

SECTION B—JUDAISM AND CHRISTIANITY ISSUES

1. *Israel and the church*—In any discussion of Judaism and Christianity, the question of Israel and the church is, of course, prominent. Those who hold to the theology of the New Testament have for the most part held to either view A or view B. but we believe there is a better view called view C.

View A—The displacement theory—In this view, *the church totally replaces Israel as the new spiritual Israel.* This is a judgment upon national Israel for its failure to accept the Messiah. All of the promises in the Tenach, which refer to Israel, such as her regathering from the nations (Isaiah 11) and the rejuvenation of her land (Isaiah 35, Ezekiel 36,37), are taken to be spiritually fulfilled in the church. For example, the abundance of the productivity of the land is taken to symbolize spiritual blessings in the church. The regathering of Israel from the four corners of the earth is interpreted as the gathering together of the saints when the Messiah returns. Usually, proponents of this view hold there will not be a literal reign of Yeshua on earth for 1,000 years, because this is presently and spiritually fulfilled in the Messiah's reign over the church.

View B—The dispensational theory—This view strongly rejects view A. It challenges the view A method of interpretation as subjective, since it does not deal with the meaning of texts according to the natural sense of their language in context. Dispensationalists believe we must interpret a text according to the author's intended meaning and as it would have been understood by the original readers. Thus, *all the Old Testament prophecies of land, regathering, and the Messiah's rule in Jerusalem, must be understood in their original sense.*

Furthermore, Romans 11:28,29 says even though the nation of Israel is an enemy of the gospel, *in regard to the election, she is elect* for the sake of her forefathers, because the gifts and call of God are irrevocable. This proves that Israel nationally is still in some sense serving a continuing, positive purpose in the plan of God. Up to this point, we strongly affirm the argument of the dispensationalists. But at this point, a strange twist is made. *Dispensationalists hold that Israel and the church are two separate peoples of God. One cannot be spiritually part of both.*

Israel serves a national earthly purpose under a covenant of law (the Mosaic and millenial orders are seen as covenants of law), whereas the church serves God under a covenant of grace (the New Covenant). Thus, when a Jew accepts Jesus in this age, his purpose is with the church, no longer with Israel.

View C—A Messianic Jewish Theory—We argue there is no such thing as a covenant of law *per se* in the Scriptures. The Mosaic order and the New Covenant order are both covenants *of grace* leading to an obedience of faith as the proper response. The New Covenant order, however, comes with a power of the Spirit, which was unavailable in the old order. This enables a fuller obedience of faith not possible before the death and resurrection of Yeshua. Furthermore, the New Covenant is promised to *the House of Israel and the House of Judah* (Jeremiah 31:31ff).

The biblical understanding of the relationship of the church to Israel is more clearly understood by the concept of commonwealth. Israel is the national center of the worldwide commonwealth under her king Yeshua.

Thus, all who become true Christians from all lands become signs of the future order of the Messiah's worldwide rule. Ephesians 2 describes them as once lost, strangers to the covenants, but now having been brought near, made recipients of the promises, and members of the commonwealth of Israel (RSV). The church has sometimes forgotten its Jewish roots and often lost sight of this, but that makes it no less true. Christians are recipients of the benefits of covenant by being under the beneficent rule of Israel's king and have all the promises of Scripture, except those which would not benefit or apply to them, such as the promise to live in the land of Israel.

The New Testament presents a mystery, previously unrevealed, that Israel the nation does not accept her own king. This can be illustrated in this way: The church is the people of God, the commonwealth, in and from all nations. Israel is the nation of God among the nations. Someday, the church will prevail and all nations, as nations, will join the commonwealth when Messiah returns.

Let's use an analogy of England under King George. Suppose England rejected the rule of King George, while the nations of the British commonwealth continued to accept his rule. There would be a British commonwealth without its central member. King George would continue to fight to reestablish his rule over England. As an Englishman, he would even say he had chosen England as the center of his rule. It is possible that the other nations in the commonwealth might feel they had *replaced* England, even though the commonwealth is rooted in England. The king, however, would have none of this talk. Even though he had established his rule in other nations, he would continue to woo and pressure England until he was finally received and could rule his empire from London. In the meantime he would extend his rule over other nations.

So it is with Yeshua the Jew. He is the rightful King of Israel. Though accepted in the commonwealth and rejected in Israel, He has chosen Israel to be His people. She is beloved for the fathers' sake and will be wooed and pressured and kept until she turns to Him. This is the prediction of Zechariah 12:10 and Romans 11:26. The king of England would not destroy or forsake his homeland. Neither would Yeshua destroy or forsake His homeland and people.

When Israel accepts her king, the commonwealth will be in the order ultimately intended for it. God's blessing will thus flow out to all nations (Zechariah 14). The great mystery of the age is that the commonwealth of Israel, under the Messiah Yeshua, is extended during this age without Israel itself being under the Messiah's rule.

This commonwealth concept has many advantages over other viewpoints.

1. It maintains a clear-headed approach which takes the Scripture in its natural sense.
2. It makes sense of God's promises to Israel.
3. It makes sense of the equality of all people of God without destroying the identity of the people of Israel proper. For example, no one would hold that an Australian is an Englishman. Yet he is no less equal under the king than an Englishman. He receives all the rights and privileges of an Englishman, being a commonwealth citizen, simply by coming under the rule of the king. Of course, he is

rooted in a system of rulership and law stemming from England, but he need not adopt specifically English celebrations and local practices.

In just such a way, Gentiles become partakers of the covenants of God with Israel. They are no longer strangers to the covenants, but *joint* heirs. Through the Messiah, they are now attached to Israel and the nourishment of the sap of the tree feeds them (Romans 11:18,24). Israel's acceptance of Yeshua's rule should be the concern of the whole commonwealth, since it will bring greater blessing to the whole commonwealth. Reading Romans 11 in the light of the commonwealth concept is a great joy; the passage speaks naturally with no violence done to its intended meaning. This fulfills the promise to Abraham that his seed (Messiah and Israel) will be the source of blessing to all nations.

2. *Gospel and law*—There is a great deal of muddled thinking concerning gospel and law in many circles. Generally, the theologians of the believing church have had much better ideas on this topic than the common person in the pew or the popular preacher. But so often the views of believing scholars do not filter down to the people. Daniel P. Fuller, the esteemed professor of biblical interpretation at Fuller Theological Seminary, has in my opinion written a definitive book on this issue. It is called *Gospel and Law.*

The problem arises basically because Messianic Jews are accused of returning to the bondage of the law when they are to live under the gospel of grace. The accusation arises because Messianic Jews celebrate the acts of God on days prescribed in the Mosaic writings. Fuller holds there is a real misunderstanding of gospel and law. He argues as follows:

a. *The word "law" in the New Testament may or may not refer to the Mosaic writings.* It may refer to Rabbinical legalism or an observed principle.

b. *Paul never argued against the commands of Scripture as being contrary to the gospel.* The gospel is the Good News that we are forgiven in Yeshua. *In Him* we are

accepted as though we had fulfilled God's law and are
empowered by the Spirit to desire to do God's commands
and be able to do them. We are freed from the bondage of
sin.

c. *Paul's argument was with a wrong approach to the law
which opposed the very heart intent of both the Mosaic
writing and the gospel. This is the approach of works-
righteousness.* Works-righteousness is the approach of
pride. Pride holds that it has by self-effort earned God's
favor. This is the opposite of the gospel which requires us
to humbly approach God as our physical healer, redeem-
er, and the one who forgives us and empowers us to obey
Him.

Our obedience is to God's glory since it is produced
by His power in us received by faith. It is not to our glory.
The attitude of the legalists in the book of Galatians
proved their approach to be one of pride and works-
righteousness. In their pride they sought to make Jews
out of the newly believing Gentiles and impose works-
righteousness on them.

d. *Paul always maintained that "all scripture . . . is profit-
able for doctrine, reproof and correction" when approached in a faith-receptive attitude of dependence on
God.* Faith and dependence on God are the opposite of
works-righteousness. The New Testament commands
can also be made into a system of works-righteousness,
as some legalistic Christian groups have done.

The question for the Messianic Jew is not whether or not he
celebrates Sabbath or Passover, as if this could be wrong. It is
rather his reason for and attitude in celebrating. Is his approach
one of thanksgiving for God's love and unmerited favor, or is it
something done in pride to gain merit before God? Is it in
obedience of faith or works-righteousness? This is a matter of
the heart.

3. *Spirit and Tradition*—Another controversy arises because many Messianic Jews maintain some of the prayer forms
and rituals of the synagogue (e.g., kissing the Torah, wearing a
tallit). There is a tacit assumption that all form is bad. But it

should be noted that nowhere does the New Testament speak against form and ritual. God, who is the same yesterday, today, and forever, used form and ritual as pictorial teaching tools in the ancient Tabernacle.

What the New Testament does teach against is having a "form of religion" while denying the power thereof. The New Testament enjoins us to allow freedom for the inspiration of the Spirit to speak through the members of the gathered community (I Corinthians 12-14). Leaders should be led by the Spirit when choosing forms. Forms must be varied to enable fresher participation by today's generation. But most of all, form should be blended with freedom so the Spirit can direct in new ways.

It is up to every person to worship with heart intent (Kavanah), whether through traditional forms, new forms, or unstructured periods. We must never think *rotely* going through form or ritual has any merit before God. At the same time forms provide continuity and pictorial lessons and basic truths are reaffirmed through them. While *formalism* is dead and contrary to the Spirit, forms are not. We must be careful in overseeing the latter so as not to fall into the former.

4. *The wall of partition*—In discussing the issue of Israel and the church, we have already touched on this concern. Ephesians chapter two teaches that Jew and Gentile are one in Yeshua. Gentiles who accept Yeshua are called the spiritual seed of Abraham. Therefore, the question arises, "By maintaining your Jewish heritage, are you not re-erecting the wall of partition which was broken down in Jesus?" The answer is obvious when we understand the meaning of the wall of partition and its various nuances.

a. *The wall refers to the barrier between Jew and Gentile in the Temple.* Gentiles were not permitted entrance to the Temple proper since they had not come under the covenant.
b. *Jews considered Gentiles unclean and their food unclean. Therefore, Rabbinical law forbade the sharing of meals with Gentiles.* Table fellowship was, in the ancient world, the key symbol of mutual acceptance.
c. *Legalists, among so-called "followers of Yeshua," re-*

*quired Gentiles to convert to Judaism before they
accepted them.* Thus circumcision became a require-
ment of fellowship, producing a false barrier to the Gentile's acceptance of the gospel.

Acts 15 settled the above issues once and for all. In Yeshua,
the Gentile is clean. Both Jew and Gentile are to bend their
scruples and desires in regard to food so they can have table
fellowship and mutual acceptance in the body of believers.
Requiring conformity for acceptance is a *wall* which hinders
fellowship. This is not a problem in Messianic congregations.
Why?

First of all, Gentiles are accepted as full members in a
Messianic congregation. Secondly, Messianic Jews maintain
fellowship with the rest of the body of believers. Culturally
diverse churches are healthy, whether black, Spanish, or Chi-
nese, as long as they open their doors to all who are called to join
them and who enjoy their expression and calling.

Requiring Jews to be like non-Jews, to forsake their cultural distinctives and conform, is *to commit the same kind of sin
which created the wall of partition.* But this time the sin would
be from the non-Jewish side in requiring conformity to non-
Jewish ways. This becomes doubly foolish when we understand the church as rooted in Israel. Jewish biblical history is
the historic background for the whole church. The Exodus and
Passover are part of the history of all the people of God rooted in
Israel, even if these events of God's grace are specifically part of
national Israel's heritage.

Messianic Jews are biblically required to maintain fellowship with the rest of God's church, and receive non-Jews as
equal members of the body. To not do so would be to *commit the
sin of re-erecting the wall of partition.*

5. *Branches of Judaism and Messianic Jews*—There are
three main branches and one minor branch of Judaism, all of
which stem from Rabbinical orthodox Judaism.

Orthodox Judaism is rooted in the first century Pharisees.
The Pharisees were one of several major sects in New Testament times. The major sects were: 1) the Sadducees, who were
closely connected to the temple system and did not believe in

the resurrection, 2) the Essenes, an ascetic sect which sought to purify Israel, 3) the Pharisees, who accepted the authority of the oral law later written down in the Talmud, 4) the Nazarenes, the followers of Yeshua and, 5) the Zealots, those whose major emphasis was political rebellion against Rome.

Yeshua's teaching contrasted with all forms of Judaism but was closer to the Pharisees and Essenes than to other sects. When Jerusalem fell, the power of other groups was diminished. The Pharisees triumphed and asserted their control over the whole community. Pharisaic Judaism was defined as the only valid Judaism and later became known as Rabbinical Judaism. Rabbinical Judaism accepted the authority of Rabbinic schools whose teaching and practice later became encoded in the Talmud. It also rejected the validity of the Messianic Jewish identity. But by fixing legal and religious dimensions for all Jews, the Rabbis did produce a continuity which aided in the preservation of Israel.

Until the Hasidic movement in the 18th century, there was no lasting major division in Talmud-based Judaism. There were varieties of schools and opinions, but nothing which produced the fierce division of Hasidism. The Hasidim were innovators, mystics, and sometimes unfortunately, magicians, who sought return to a freer, personalized expression of Judaism. They danced and broke out of prescribed forms. But over the years, the Hasidic movement tempered and became more classically orthodox. During the height of the division, the leaders of the traditional Jews excommunicated the Hasidic leaders. But this rift is no longer the division which prevailed in the 18th century.

The rise of modern science, enlightenment philosophy, and the desire for a more culturally adapted Judaism, spurred the movement of Reform Judaism in Germany, England, and the United States. At first, Reform sought to adapt the tradition to a new age. Many Reform Jews still believed in God, immortality, and social ethics, but they removed talmudic strictures and modernized Jewish liturgy. But Reform turned more and more radical until it became anti-Zionist, and even secular-humanist in some orientations.

Some Reform congregations tried to make Judaism a modern religion for all peoples, not a national religion. Since the holocaust, many in the Reform movement have adopted more tradition and have become Zionists, believing in the value and place of Israel the nation. Within Reform, there is still a great deal of secular influence, agnosticism, and humanism in regard to religious truth.

When Reform drifted more radically from traditional roots, conservatives split from their ranks forming conservative Judaism. They wanted reform from orthodoxy, but in a more conservative, less radical way. Religious beliefs among conservatives vary widely. Reconstructionism is a movement which is conservative in religious tradition, but secular-humanist in religious belief.

Since most Judaism today, except for Messianic Judaism and Karaitism,* is rooted in Rabbinical Judaism, all have adopted the tradition of rejecting the Messianic Jewish option. Various branches of Judaism may be more or less tied to the authority of Rabbinic Judaism (e.g., Reform claims to be rooted in the prophetic social justice tradition more than in the Rabbinic), but all branches accept the judgment of the Pharisees against Messianic Jews. Messianic Jews must be strong and not let the authority of men preclude their biblically rooted identity in Yeshua.

    6. *Siddur, Halachah, Kabbalah*

    a. *The Siddur* is the Jewish prayer book. The material in the Siddur was compiled over a period of 1,800 years. Some material parallels Yeshua in basic content. The Messianic Jew should respect the material of the Siddur since:

      1. Eighty percent is either direct Scriptural quotation or creative intertwining of Scripture passages.

      2. Fifteen percent is prayer material inspired by Scripture.

      3. Only a very small portion contains anything contrary to biblical faith.

---

* Karaites: Those who rejected Talmud and Rabbinic tradition and root their practice in Torah alone.

This material is a great resource for worship, whether used
traditionally or as a sourcebook for new worship songs and
prayers.

b. *Halachah* is the application of biblical law and Rabbinical tradition to new situations. Halachah is the legal
tradition of Judaism. England and the United States
have legal traditions as do most nations. However, Halachah regulated personal, social, religious and national
life among Jews. Messianic Jews should recognize the
value of tradition which applies principles to new situations, but should be aware of these cautions:

1. The claim that the original Halachic material (the
Talmud) is an Oral Law given to Moses by God, is
spurious and without historical foundation. It is true
some of the Oral traditions in the Talmud are ancient,
even possibly from applications made during Mosaic
times, but much is clearly from situations in first century times. The claim that Rabbinical methods of
interpreting the Bible produce conclusions which
rediscover the Oral Law is also spurious.

2. Some of the applications in the Jewish tradition are
excellent, but some are contrary to the New Testament. Scripture must always be our source for eval-
uating later applications.

3. We must never accept the Jewish tradition as having
a binding force over our lives, just because it is
tradition.

c. *Kaballah* is the Jewish mystical tradition found in the
Zohar and other writings. The mystical traditions are
truly a "mixed bag." Hasidic Judaism is deeply involved
in this tradition. It has become fashionable in many
Jewish circles to be favorable toward the mystical traditions. Is this a Jewish response to the influence of Eastern religions? In the Kabbalah one finds marvelous
meditations on such things as the Messiah's atoning
death and the triune nature of God. But one also finds
dangerous *magical* occult traditions which Gershom
Scholem (*Major Trends in Jewish Mysticism*) shows
stem from second century paganisms.

The Messianic Jew benefits from and must have a *discerning respect for* and *understanding of* Jewish history, movements, and traditions. He should be cautious in his affirmation and rejections, always submitting his thinking to the Word and the Spirit.

STUDY QUESTIONS

1. Define the three views of the relationship between Israel and the church given in our summary.

   a. _____

   _____

   _____

   b. _____

   _____

   _____

   c. _____

   _____

   _____

2. Fuller's view on gospel and law primarily argues four major points of interpretation. They are:

   a. _____

   _____

   _____

   b. _____

_____

_____

c. _____

_____

d. _____

_____

_____

3. What is the wall of partition? Give three parts of the meaning of this phrase.

a. _____

_____

_____

b. _____

_____

_____

c. _____

_____

_____

4. Do Messianic Jews re-erect the wall of partition? Explain.

_____

_____

_____

_____

5. Name and describe the following:

   a. Reform Judaism _____

   _____

   _____

   b. Conservative Judaism _____

   _____

   _____

   c. The Siddur _____

   _____

   _____

   d. Halachah _____

   _____

   _____

   e. Kabbalah _____

   _____

   _____

VERSES FOR MEMORIZATION

Romans 3:31   Ephesians 3:12-14   Ephesians 3:19

SECTION C—THE FUTURE

The New Testament begins with the announcement of the Kingdom of God. Truly, in Yeshua, the kingdom or rule of God has come. However, the rule of God through His people has not yet come in fullness. The Kingdom of God is now extended in the worldwide growth of the body of believers, but the Kingdom of God will be extended over all the earth when the Messiah returns. As predicted in Isaiah 9:7, His rule shall not have boundaries, He shall rule on the throne of David. However, before this rule is established, many events must first take place.

It is not wise to try and derive a detailed scenario of the future from Scripture, but there is a broad general outline which is clear. In the present, we can say, the Kingdom has come in Yeshua, but it is yet to come in its fullness at His return. Before His return we expect these events:

1. The Bible predicts *the re-gathering of Israel* in unbelief. They will exist as a nation, but only fully turn to Him at His return (Zechariah 12:10).

2. The desert will blossom as a rose and Israel will prosper (Isaiah 35, Ezekiel 36).

3. After Israel's re-establishment, there will be a *turning of the nations of the world against Israel.* We can see this already taking place today.

4. *A northern confederacy,* probably led by Soviet Russia, will lead an invasion of Israel only *to be roundly defeated* on the mountains of Israel by Israel and the European confederacy. We are not dogmatic about Russia's invasion before the final battle, but this seems to make the best sense of Scripture. (See Ezekiel 38,39. The student should read these chapters.)

5. *A European confederacy is spoken of as a ten-horned (ten nation) beast* in Daniel seven and as the last great World Empire in the image Daniel saw in Daniel 2 (the toes of iron and clay).

6. *Out of this tremendous war will arise a new leader who promises peace and order. He is the Anti-Christ,* spoken of as the little horn (Daniel 7). Paul taught the Anti-Christ would make his appearance before the Messiah returns (II Thessalonians 2). During his rulership, which is pervasive over all the

world, though strongest in Europe, he will seek absolute control. He will seek an obedience and honor due only to God. This will lead to the persecution of the church and of Israel, who will resist this infringement of power.

7. *The Anti-Christ will have control over economic transactions which computer technology makes possible today.* Only those who pledge loyalty, and receive his mark will be free (Revelation 13:16-17).

8. *Israel will resist this perversion* and the Anti-Christ's forces will invade Israel. However, just when it looks as though his forces will win, the Messiah will return in the clouds of glory and defeat him fully.

(The student should read Matthew 24, Mark 13, Luke 17 and 21 to gain insight into this period while keeping in mind some details refer to the destruction of Jerusalem in the first century.)

Other events pointing to the end are also listed in these passages and in Revelation:

a. wars and rumors of wars
b. more frequent earthquakes
c. amazing forces of military destruction
d. rampant immorality
e. 144,000 Jewish believers who witness to the truth before the world (Revelation 7)
f. a powerful witness for the gospel in all nations as the church uses these events as signs to point people to the truth (Revelation 7,14)
g. great martyrdom for the sake of witness (we are assured, however, the saints will prevail).

After these events, the Messiah will raise those who have died. In I Thessalonians 4:16,17,18 we are told to comfort mourners with the words of this wonderful text:

"For the Lord Himself will come down from heaven, with a loud command, with the voice of the archangel and with the trumpet call of God, and the dead in Messiah will rise first. After that, we who are

still alive and are left will be caught up together with
them in the clouds to meet the Lord in the air. And so
we will be with the Lord forever. Therefore encourage each other with these words."

Actually, the Scriptural view of the last days is not for the
purpose of satisfying our curiosity about the details of the
future events. Instead, the Biblical emphasis is to exhort the
followers of Yeshua to fulfill their destiny by fulfilling their
calling and thus "hastening the day" of His coming. (II Peter
3:12).

Indeed, beyond the scenario of events broadly outlined
above, Scripture makes it clear that before Yeshua returns His
followers will be restored to unity and power (John 17:21). This
was the prayer of Yeshua before His death and we believe it
will be answered! This unity, power and love precede our
transformation as a body to be with him ("that they may be
where I am," John 17:24).

This unified and restored body will have given powerful
loving witness to Israel before the Messiah's return, for we
read in Romans 11 that Israel will receive the mercy of God
through the mercy shown them by the Gentile believers.
(Romans 11:31). The Gentiles are to so demonstrate the love,
power and mercy of God in signs, wonders and practical deeds
of love, that Israel will be made desirous of her own Messiah!
(Romans 11:13-14).

Paul also noted that one Key to Israel's salvation in
addition to this Gentile witness, is the witness of the part of
Israel that is saved. (Romans 11:14, 15). He is concerned that
part of Israel be saved, for this will lead to all Israel being
saved. Only if there is a significant minority of Jewish
believers, is it a real possibility for all of Israel to turn to
Yeshua. *Hence both the witness of the whole church and the
Messianic Jew who is still recognizably part of Israel is crucial
if Israel is to be saved.*

Israel's salvation is the key end time event along with the
Gospel of the Kingdom being proclaimed to all nations. For
Paul notes of Israel that their full acceptance will lead to "life
from the dead." (Romans 11:15). Yeshua states that the end

will come when the Gospel of the Kingdom has been preached in all the world as a witness (Matt. 24:13). However, earlier, He *connected His return to* Israel's leaders (Jerusalem) turning and saying to Yeshua, "Blessed is he that comes in the name of the Lord." (Matthew 23:29).

This corporate turning to Yeshua opens the way for the nations to repent after the defeat of those that come against Israel (Zechariah 14). Thence, all nations will send representatives to keep the feast of Sukkoth and the world wide Kingdom of God will be established in fullness. (Zechariah 14).

It is crucial to note therefore that the future, including world evangelization, Israel's salvation, and the return of the Messiah, are contingent in part upon believers in Yeshua fulfilling their calling!

In summary, before Messiah's return Israel as a whole nation will call upon Yeshua saying, "Blessed is he who comes in the name of the Lord." (Matthew 23:29). "They will mourn for Him whom they have pierced and will as a nation be saved." (Matthew 23:39, Romans 11:26).

At the time of the first resurrection, only those who were saved before Messiah's coming will be resurrected. They will appear before His judgment seat and receive their reward according to their life of faith (II Corinthians 5:10). Then they will be transformed into resurrection bodies like the Messiah Yeshua. We will be like Him.

> "Listen, I tell you a mystery: We will not all sleep, but we will all be changed—in a flash, in the twinkling of an eye, at the last trumpet. For the trumpet will sound, and the dead will be raised imperishable, and we will all be changed." (I Corinthians 15:51,52)

It is important to realize Scripture's picture of our future perfection is not the image of disembodied spirits or souls. Our future existence will be a bodily existence, but this body will not be imperfect or subject to disease. It will be like the resurrection body of Messiah (I Corinthians 15:42-44).

The Messiah will return to earth with all His resurrected followers. The reign of evil will be utterly vanquished and the nations who have come against Israel will be defeated in the battle of Armageddon in central Israel. This will commence the worldwide reign of the Messiah. As predicted in the Bible, He will rule on the throne of His father David and His Kingdom shall know no boundaries (Isaiah 9:6-7).

Revelation 20:1-6 tells us the Messiah *will seize Satan and bind him for 1,000 years* by throwing him into the Abyss and sealing it over him. The saints will then reign with the Messiah for this 1,000 year period known as the millennium. During this time, the commonwealth of Israel under the Messiah Yeshua will extend over all the earth.

The nature of the millennium is described in the prophets. *Nature will produce abundantly.* The people who enter the millennium without having repented before the Messiah's return, but who repented at His return, will live a life characterized by longevity. To die at 100 will be considered as dying in one's youth. This will be a period of discipline and learning for the whole human race. I believe *lessons will be taught concerning justice, stewardship of the resources of the earth, and the nature of society built on respect, cooperation, sharing, and responsibility.*

We read in Zechariah 14 that all nations will send representatives to celebrate the feast of Sukkoth (Tabernacles) and in Isaiah 66 that all will live a cycle of life related to Sabbath and New Moon. Since national-cultural and legal barriers will be removed (which previously might have been a hardship to non-Jewish believers), *all will enjoy the Sabbath and Sukkoth.* Thus the original cycle of life built around the history of God's gracious acts will be observed worldwide. However, all will point to and celebrate the Messiah's work. *Ezekiel 40-48 probably describes worship in the millenial Temple which will be a great commonwealth institution* for memorializing the Messiah's death, resurrection, and kingship.

At the end of this 1,000-year transition period, there will be oone last rebellion. Satan will be loosed and many will follow him. How can this be? (cf. Revelation 20:7-10).

1. It is important to note that those who are still living in natural bodies and who come to birth and die during this period may or may not accept the Messiah in heart, even if

they are externally forced to accept His rule.

2. It is probable that the Messiah and the saints will withdraw their strong, direct rule, and delegate authority to the other still unresurrected humans. Evil-hearted people will be able to rationalize their rebellion against their authorities. This is especially likely when Satan dazzles with his power and false delusion of beauty and light.

This last rebellion will be utterly crushed, ushering in the final judgment and the new heavens and new earth. This last judgment will consign all of the lost to final doom. However, it will be a time of resurrection to life for those who died in faith during the millenial age.

We read that all are to be judged according to their works (Revelation 20:13). Were they works of faith-obedience or works of fleshly pride and sin? Those whose names are in the Book of Life are saved for eternity. Of the rest we read:

> "Then death and Hades were thrown into the lake of fire. the lake of fire is the second death. If anyone's name was not found written in the Book of Life, he was thrown into the lake of fire." (vs 14,15)

Revelation 20 and 21 commences with the most marvelous description of the new heavens and new earth which will at this time come into being. We believe the new heavens and new earth are in continuity with God's original creation, but reflect a total renewal. The New Jerusalem will be established at this time. The description in Revelation 20 and 21 is truly wonderful. God shall wipe away every tear, and joy in the presence of God will be our portion.

(The student should read Revelation 20 through 22 at this point.)

In the light of this, how should we then live? The issues of our eternal destiny are at stake and determined on the basis of our response to the Good News of redemption in Yeshua. The lake of fire awaits the unrepentant, but the New Jerusalem awaits the saved. Thus, we must live lives dedicated to holy living and prayerfully seek to win the lost to the Kingdom of

God. We must learn to effectively share our wonderful faith with others.

Now that we know the basics we need to ask why God has left us on earth. Our purpose is to be a light, a witness to what God has done for us in Yeshua. Failure in this regard destroys the joy of our faith. Faith is a gift to be shared! Our most effective witness is our own testimony of what God has done for us, along with a clear presentation of the Good News. Prayerfully, we need to ask God to lead us to those with whom we can share our faith. Messianic Jews have a special burden for Israel. If we pray and are sensitive to the Spirit, we will be frequently led to those with whom we can share.

The best way to learn to witness can be summarized in two steps: (1) Observe and walk with someone who is a successful witness. (2) Do it. Open your mouth in faith. Our witness is in *deed* and *word*. Seek to serve your neighbors, friends, and family with the love of the Messiah. Invite them to your fellowship. May God bless your Spirit-led efforts!

We have come to the end of our basic course in Messianic Jewish discipleship and our last section of study questions and verses for memorization follow. Remember, this course is only a first step in growth and understanding. We exhort you to stay in the Word and give yourself to the reading of solid spiritual books. (Lists of basic advanced books follow this section). Grow with God! May He bless your life richly.

STUDY QUESTIONS

1. List the eight major events which precede the Messiah's Second Coming.

   a. _____

   b. _____

   c. _____

   d. _____

e. _____

f. _____

g. _____

h. _____

2. When the Messiah returns:

a. What will happen to those who have died in Yeshua? ___

_____

_____

_____

b. What will Israel do? _____

_____

_____

_____

3. The Messiah's return will usher in the millenial .age. Describe several features of this 1,000-year period.

a. _____

b. _____

c. _____

d. _____

e. _____

4. At the end of the millennium, Satan will be loosed.

a. The nations will _____

_____

_____

b. The Messiah will _____

_____

_____

c. This will lead to the last judgment in which _____

_____

_____

5. The final end of all things is the _____

_____

_____

described in Revelation 21 and 22.

VERSES FOR MEMORIZATION
I Thessalonians 4:16-18
I Corinthians 15:3-6
I Corinthians 15:51-52

FOR FURTHER READING

From Sabbath To Sunday	Bacchiocchi, S.
Everyman's Talmud	Cohen, A. (Dr.)
The Theology of Jewish Christianity	Danielou, J.
Gospel and Law, Contrast or Continuum	Fuller, Daniel
A History of the Jews	Grayzel, Solomon
The Jewish People and Jesus Christ	Jocz, Jakob
Jewishness and Jesus	Juster, Daniel
The Fig Tree Blossoms	Loberman, Paul
Biblical Exegesis in the Apostolic Period	Longenecker, R.
A Rabbinic Anthology	Montefiore, C.G.
Foundations	Prince, D.